Evoloving

Poetry and Photography
By James Fly

Amazing Things Press

Book design by Julie L. Casey

ISBN 978-0615974699

Printed in the United States of America.

For more information, visit

www.jamesfly.weebly.com
or
www.amazingthingspress.com

Table of Contents
Introduction

The Rhythm and the Rhyme

Poems
Section 1: Love

Section 2: Life

Section 3: Nature

Section 4: Current Events

Photographs

"The bird cannot fly, until it breaks the shell."

~India.Arie from her cd *SongVersation*

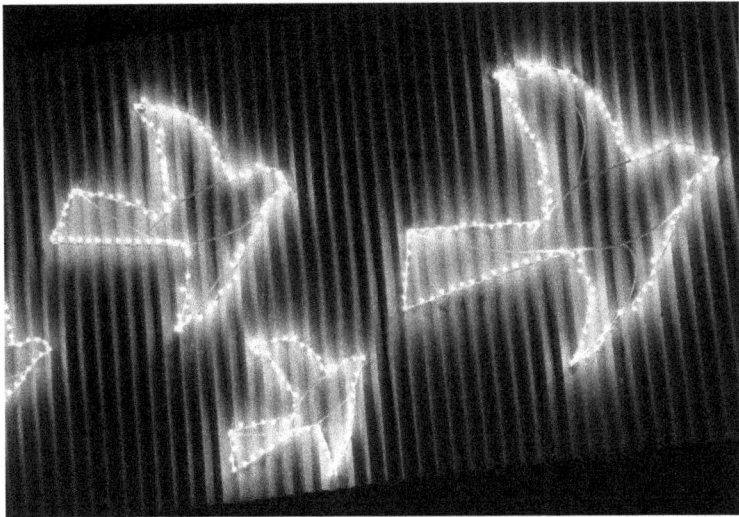

Introduction

The Rhythm and the Rhyme

I grew up in a matriarchal household during my formative years. It consisted of myself, my mother, my aunt and my maternal grandmother Lillian Fly because my father was away at sea in the Navy. I trace my love of poetry to sitting on the laps of my "three mothers" as they read Mother Goose Nursery rhymes to me. They were so simple and yet often profound with life lessons. Later, I learned to love "grownup" nursery rhymes by the likes of Emily Dickinson and Robert Frost, who remain two of my favorite poets. I also appreciate the power and simplicity of Carl Sandburg's verse, as well as the great lyricists of Broadway musicals, both past and present, plus contemporary singer-songwriters. I have also been greatly influenced by the poetic beauty and majesty of Biblical verses, in particular First Corinthians 13, the Apostle Paul's immutable tribute to Love. Any poems about love, in fact, are "seen through a glass darkly" compared to the clarity of this unbreakable mirror... Another inspiration was my Great Uncle Oscar Gibson, my mother's uncle, who self published *Verse from the River of Years* at the end of his long ministerial career. Uncle Oscar was truly one of the most happy and inspirational people I have ever known, always ready to impart his wisdom to others with gentleness and good humor. My paternal Grandmother, Lillian Fly, was also a writer. She once had an interview with Walt Disney about the possibility of dramatizing her life growing up in a sod house on the Kansas prairie. A special education teacher in Whittier, California, she carried a camera with her wherever she went and on travels with her as a young boy, I learned to appreciate the visual as well as the verbal. In the ninth grade, my English teacher at Mile High Academy in Denver required all of his students to memorize and recite famous poems in front of the class. I remember my assignments were "O Captain,

1

My Captain" and "The Highwayman" and I still recall parts of each poem to this day.

There are so many other people to thank for inspiring me to write this book, whether they realize it or not. First would be my dear wife, Connie, this Lone Ranger's faithful Tonto, who inspired several of these poems, my three sons, Eric, Ryan and Hans, and many friends and acquaintances I encounter on a daily basis. As fellow IIN graduate and life and health coach Cora Poage of Brooklyn, N.Y. puts it, "Life is poetry." Indeed, it is. Finally, a very special tribute to Julie Casey, owner and publisher of Amazing Things Press. Breaking out of my shell and reading that first poem at the St. Joseph Writers' Guild and meeting the dedicated and talented Julie there, made this book possible.

The poems (and most of the photos taken) in *Evoloving* were written over a two-year period and reflect an awakening personal philosophy and spirituality based on observation and experience. Poetry has become the way I process life. I believe we are all on this planet to learn how to love ourselves and each other more and more. That is our "soul purpose." Photography has been called visual jazz and to me poetry is verbal music. My poetry is not avant garde or surrealistic and you don't need a degree in the Classics to understand it. It is simple and perspicuous (clearly expressed and presented). Hopefully, it is also thought-provoking. May the reader be rocked by the rhythm and the rhyme.

~James Fly, St. Joseph, Missouri, April 2014

Red Balloon

a red balloon
rises skyward,

a helium vagrant
from sleeping fingers

released
from the carnival of faces
staring in the park.

The widow
wonders where it is going,

the clown
wonders when it will pop,

and a child is crying
because she knows
and wonders how it
tugged

deceptively

away.

Written by James Fly, age 10

Section 1

Love

Only Love

Only love can generate
Only love can pulsate
Only love can circulate
the blood of love inviolate.

Resonance Image

My heart reflects yours
as yours mirrors mine,
We join and divide
as a double Valentine—
Sometimes the mimic
and sometimes the mime...

Genuine Valentine

If I could send the world a Valentine,
a heart that would never cease to shine,
I wouldn't send Hallmark cards
with flattering or flowery words.
I'd send something better than the very best
from the caring center of peace and rest.
I'd tell everyone to look inside
for there and there alone they'll find
the Valentine that's genuine...
Why look to others for self respect?
They have their own egos to protect
and you're the one they'll most neglect,
and if not neglect,
abuse you,
and if not abuse, use you
for their own agenda,
or at the very least, try to change you,
but you can only change yourself;
it's not the job description of anyone else.
True love accepts you as you are,
it never dims your luminous star.

When it comes to age or gender,
it doesn't really matter
whether son or daughter,
toddler or elder—
until you love yourself as a mother loves her child
and a child loves its mother,
there's no way in the world
you can fully love another,
cherish sister, care for brother.
When you love your essence
lived fully in the present
no one's dis can ever dismiss
your beautiful, magical presence.
So, from the beginning to the end
you have to become your own best friend:
the soul mate who will never leave you,
the one who will always receive you;
the one who will always believe you,
the one who will never deceive you...
Yes, if I could send the world a Valentine,
a heart that would never cease to shine,
I'd tell everyone to look inside
connecting to the Great Divine
for there and there alone they'll find
the Valentine that's genuine.

Love Life

Love life
with every breath
work and play
take time to rest
living life
is not a test
it's a pearl
a priceless gift.

Love life
do your best
find a way
to use your gift
live your life
not to impress
but to serve
and to be blessed.

Love life
and don't forget
to mean what you say
so they won't have to guess
your real intentions
with no regrets.

Love life
don't fear death
it's a day
for you to rest
when you've taken
your final breath
and you've given the last
of your very best...

Love Speaks

Love doesn't always spin cotton candy sweetness
or turn the other cheek in subservient meekness.
Sometimes love looks flint-eyed hard,
answering back with an amplified word
just to make its own voice heard.

It's not that love means to be uncouth,
but in all that matters,
love never flatters,
for love above all
speaks the truth.

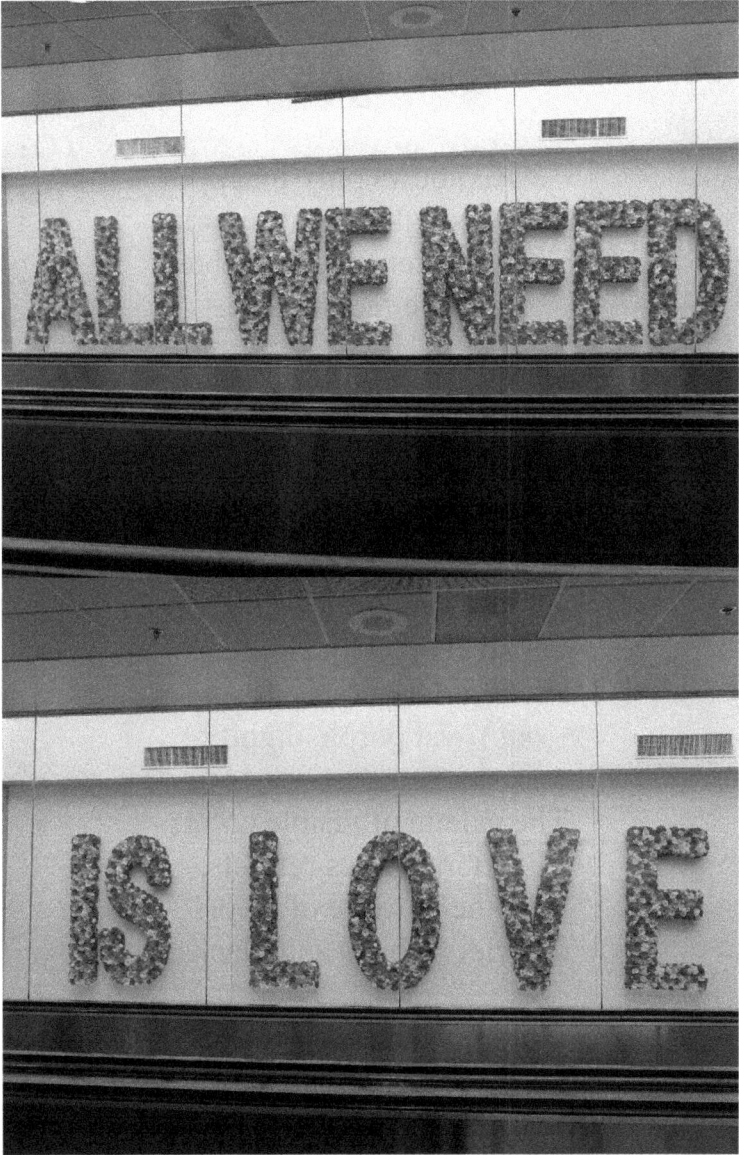

Colors of Love

Rainbows only form
when sunlight shines on rain,
and love remains invisible
until we feel its pain.

And then we see the colors
we couldn't see before,
the spectrum of emotions
in the prism of our core,

Refracted in our heartfelt tears
so everyone can see
the scarlet of our passion,
our royal purple dignity.

The palette of visible colors
in vibrant hues refracts,
save the absence of color—
colorless whites and blacks.

To see them all at once
makes us realize
we can only see and feel love
when we open up our eyes...

The Eyes Have It...

Only in the eyes
reflects no surprise.
The lips may deceive
and make you believe
the disingenuous play.
But a steady gaze
or a furtive glance
unmask the soul
leaving nothing to chance
like deceitful gradations of gray...

Languages of Love

He gives her a gift
a diamond cut fine
but she would much rather
that he gave her time.

She tells him she loves him
emphasizes how much
but he wants to feel the caress
of her touch.

So he slips up behind her
in wraparound embrace
but she would just like him
to fix up the place.

They speak the same language
but their dialects and words
get lost in translation
and not really heard.

If they could speak less
and listen more to each other
they might understand

the mother tongue of lovers...

Waves of Goodbye

That ship has sailed,
lines loosed from the port
it's not time to abandon ship
or abort
the voyage
or reset the clock—
you wouldn't find the same person
standing on the dock.

They've waved goodbye
and bid you farewell:
you must sail onward,
meet the oncoming swell.
waves of the hand from the person on land
meet the waves of the seas in saltwater breeze

Someday you'll find someone to match your ardor
waiting for you in a distant harbor...

Half and Whole

Two halves don't make a whole.
In fact, they dig the deepest hole
in any relationship,
turning intimacy into gamesmanship—
an unsatisfactory arrangement
and divisive estrangement.
You are whole within yourself;
you're not the better half of someone else
and they're not the part of you that's missing:
You are free to make your own decisions
in a kingdom where you reign as sovereign,
endowed with authority to lovingly govern.
But when two wholes meet each other
and decide as partners to join together
their bond becomes stronger
and their union lasts longer
than those who try to supply the lack:
the perception that they're only half.

So are you whole or are you half?
Only you can do the math.

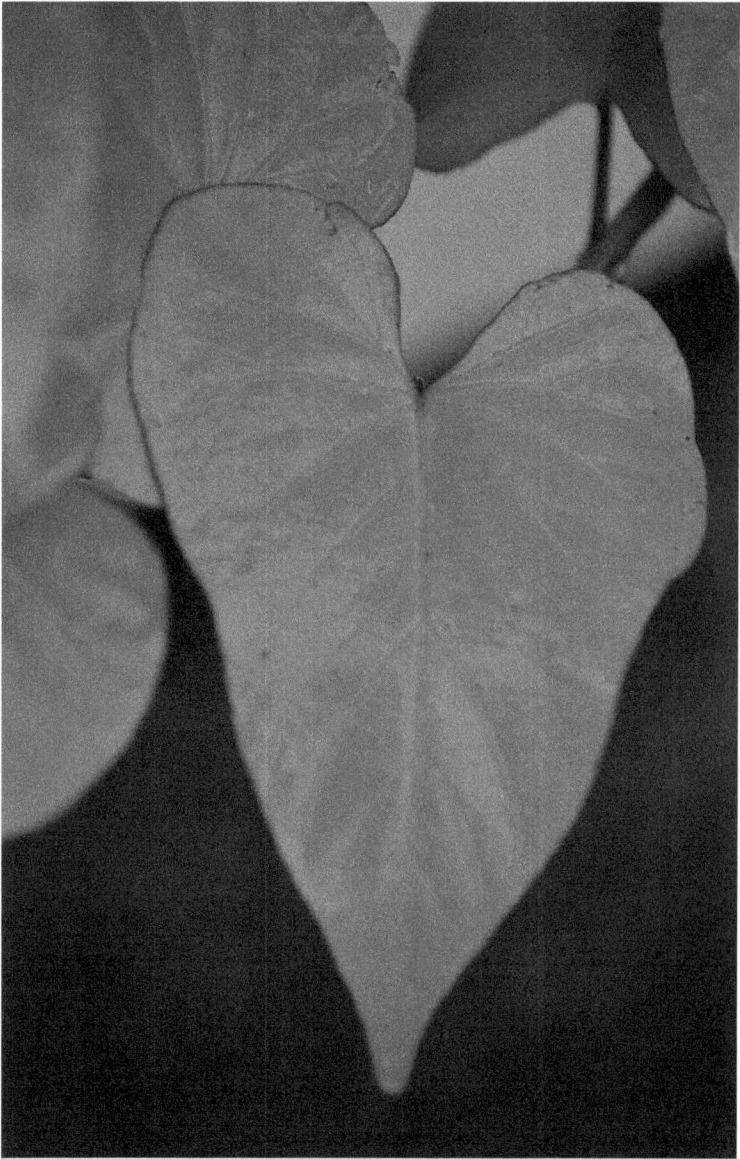

Seeds of Love

Sow seeds of love
instead of weeds of hate.

Compassion and tolerance,
unconditional benevolence
are the ones to cultivate.

We might never know
if the seeds of love we sow
ever germinate and grow

That's not up to us
to differentiate.
It really all depends, you see
on the agricultural trinity:
the falling of the rain
the shining of the sun
and the soil in which they're sown...

Living Our Loving

Living our loving,
finally moving
out of striving
into giving,
from competing to cooperating,
no longer longing for possessing
or obsessing about controlling
or even doing
but simply just being:
laughing and crying
shining light to the dying
and never denying
the worth of our birthing—
not just looking but really seeing
and not only hearing
but also listening,
yearning for learning
and earning for meaning
and always believing in progressing,
distancing ourselves from regressing;
never cursing but always blessing,
parenting without dominating
and ever remembering
when we're surrendering
into living our loving,
we're loving our living...

Inside Insight

Love walks beside us
holds our hands to guide us
but then lets go
to let us know
love always lives inside us.

Evoloving

love glows and radiates
love flows and emanates
love knows and pulsates
the throbbing heart of the universe
orbiting its elliptical course,
evolving over time and space
born in the infinite infant
of the human race.
consciously unconscious
until the instant
it sees itself
mirrored in another's face...

Evolove

Evolove:
an impeccable palindrome--
growing forward in love
and returning to its home.

Luminheiries

We have descended from the stars,
made of celestial dust Divine
and in our hearts burns a sacred fire
for we were created to let love shine,
claiming our birthright as Luminheiries
radiating now
throughout all time...

You Too

I love you,
indeed, I do,
and it's only because
I love Me too.
How about you?
Do you love you too?

Cover Up

We cover up each other
in the winter when it's colder,
a blanket on the shoulder
comforts like a mother.
We no longer need to smother
in the summer now we're older
and comfort seems to smolder
in this winterlude for lovers.

Attractions and Actions

I am attracted to many
but won't act on any
for I am committed
and won't be acquitted
for infidelity.
With a warm embrace
I feel nurtured
but anything more might be misinterpreted.
So when I'm in a woman's presence
I contemplate her essence
and form fades to obscurity.
I'm persuaded oxytocin
makes a friendlier potion
than sensuality.

Love's Flavor

You can't taste love but you can feel love,
a sixth-sense flavor love is made of,
Every cookie ever baked
will lose its flavor
if not baked
in the ovens above...

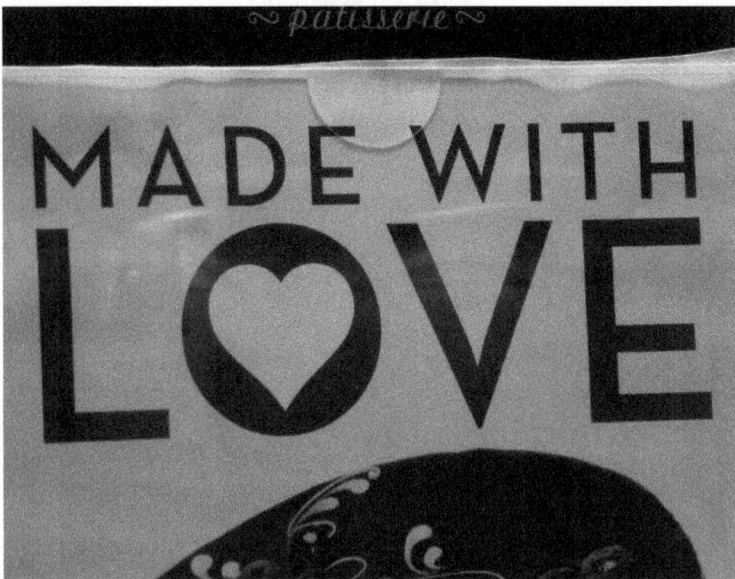

Lovers' Eyes

You say you see me with a full head of hair
even though
we both know,
like the Emperor's new clothes
there's nothing there.

I trace the outline of your young-girl figure
but when you look at yourself in the mirror
you view the reflection of another
perhaps someone resembling your mother.

We have come to see each other
through aging's disguise
with the clearer vision
of lovers' eyes...

They Could be Us

Don't slip up
make sure to share love
it's the litmus test
of our true makeup.

Because love is more than a warm fuzzy feeling—
It's bandaging a wound when someone is bleeding
and when they're hungry
cooking food and feeding,
covering them when they're cold
protecting them when they're old.

When a person or animal in time of need
comes to us with eyes that plead
scarcely able to believe
that someone will care
someone will heed
someone's heart will actually bleed,
don't slip up
make sure to share love
the next time around
they could be us...

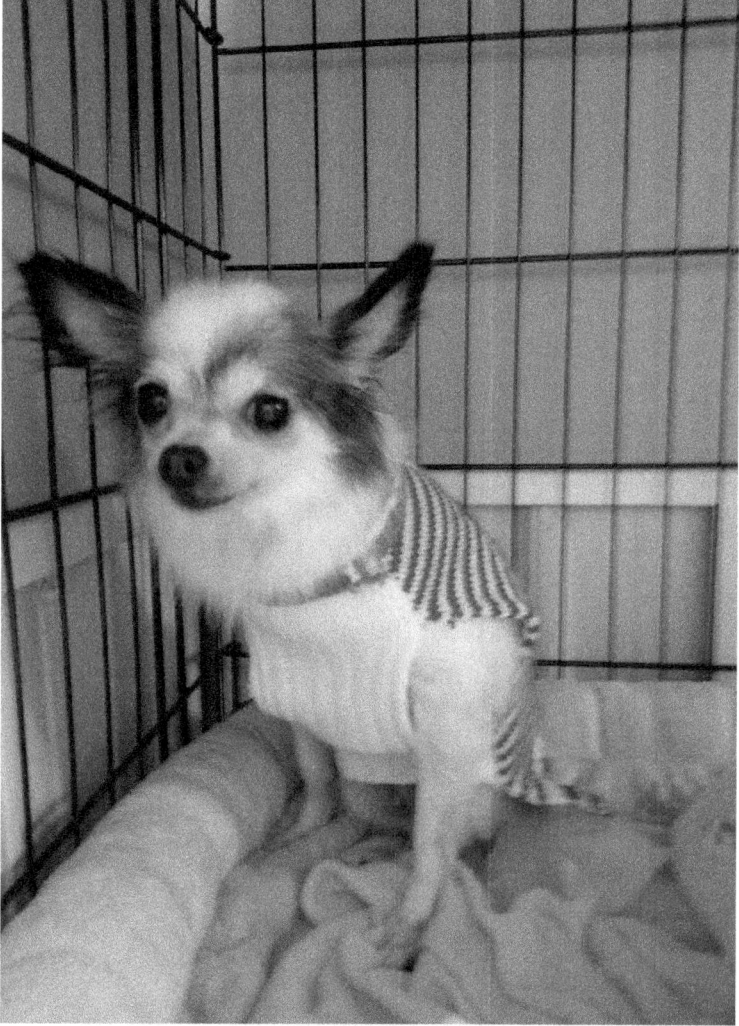
Photo by Kim Blake

She Sent Me Flowers

She sent me flowers
on the anniversary of our first date.
Back then, we could only anticipate
the direction our relationship would take.
Her intention was not to obligate
and for once I did not reciprocate.

A true love believer,
through the years
she's made me believe her
that sometimes it's okay
to just be the receiver
and in that regard
I'm giving her the pleasure
of loving her significant other.

She telephoned the florist,
"I want to send flowers
I know he really loves colors
but make sure the arrangement is masculine—
feminine is just not him."

When the flowers were delivered that day
I instinctively knew that this bouquet
blossomed from the heart of someone
who loves me more than anyone
who's not afraid to take the lead
who's never been a traitor

and I would never trade her
because I don't always have to be

love's initiator...

The Color and the Name

Love has a color and a name
Sacred red agape burns as flame
and in its light no shadow cast of shame
for love forever, it can never change...

Section 2

Life

Life is Poetry

Life is poetry:
It's the metaphor and simile
of comedy and tragedy
and mundane daily normalcy.
It's anthropomorphic hyperbole—
Dr. Doolittle's
talking menagerie.

It's parable and allegory
representing the human story.
It's onomatopoeia
the whisper and the howl
when sounds become words
like guttural and growl.
It's assonance and alliteration
vowels and consonants
in constant rotation.
It's the unmetered rhythm of free verse
unrhymed and out of time
word upon word
line upon line.
From Whitman's depiction of the ship of state
to Dickinson's position for heaven's gate
and Kilmer's rhapsody to the lovely tree
life is simply poetry
it's living and loving
it's losing and learning
it's you
and it's me.

One and Done

The way we do anything
is the way we do everything,
but if we try to do everything,
we can do nothing.

So just do something;
do one thing—one
and anything becomes everything
done...

The African American Haberdasher

He walked with style and a certain verve,
he dressed above the sartorial curve,
an ambassador for designer hats and scarves—
the African American haberdasher
in his shop at Hallmark's exclusive Crown Center.

Proud owner of both Kangols and Stetsons,
an English derby was his prized possession.
"Try it on," he offered with singular intention
"and you, sir, will be a man of distinction."
He doffed his derby, looked me straight in the eye,
his eight-ball skull matched the cueball of mine.—
the African American haberdasher
in his shop at Hallmark's exclusive Crown Center.

"Even the gangstas in the twenties and thirties
wore hats and suits, nothin' torn or dirty—
why Al Capone wouldn't be shot dead
wearin' the saggy pants of rapper threads.
A man's not fully dressed till a hat's on his head,
that, my friend, is the standard of measure,"
he said in a voice as soft as calfskin leather.

For this sophisticated ebony gentleman
with features as fine as a polished mandolin
dress manifests the wardrobe within.
For him proper dress was a necessary pleasure
and his collection of hats his particular treasure,
the crown of his closet which without acquisition
would constitute a serious wardrobe

46

malfunction.—
the African American haberdasher
in his shop at Hallmark's exclusive Crown Center.

"I only own four baseball caps but I rarely wear
them,"
"Neither do I, so what are they for then?"
"They're for baseball games—
you wear a hat to fit the occasion—
a derby to church or maybe to shows equestrian."
He bemoaned the fact that modern dress
had rumpled into sloppiness.
Could he be related to Carroll's Mad Hatter?
Yet I had to admit he looked exceedingly
dapper.—
The African American haberdasher
in his shop at Hallmark's exclusive Crown Center.

We tipped our hats as I turned to go,
he winked slyly at me with a slight little bow,
"You gotta wear a hat to be the star of the show,
that's really the trademark of a man in the know."
said the African American haberdasher
in his shop at Hallmark's exclusive Crown Center.
I realized then what he was telling me,
why he emphasized especially
that a balding guy's head's not complete sans
chapeau—
it's the masculine wig of the hairless ego!

Michael Miller, owner of "The Missing Piece" located
In Crown Center, Kansas City, Missouri

Punctyouation

Our lives are marked by punctuation,
the highest points of exclamation!
the pauses of commas,
myriads of periods.
hyphens-of-connection
apostrophes' of possession,
and colons of emphasis:
(But only a parenthesis)
makes sense of the sentences...

Now

the past is past
it didn't last
and good or bad
we can't change it.
the future is future
it's not here yet
and light or dark,
we can't arrange it.
Now ignites the torch
that illuminates the present
now burns eternity's singular moment...

Bleak Friday

the very day after
and now the day of
giving thanks for the things we need,
we storm the beachheads of corporate
and consumer greed.
Armed with plastic,
we seek bargains fantastic
for the latest digital gadgetry
and ultimate connectivity.
Forgetting in our frenzied plans
that only as we clasp our hands
together
around Thanksgiving's table
are we truly able
to relate authentically...

Body Burdens

The body bears the burdens of the past—
the smirk
the snub
the cocked-back fist:
tattoos on the soul
we can't seem to erase.

Drugs and counseling can't take the place
of nurturing our inner child face to face.

The pain of childhood molestation
layers on layers of adult insulation
stunting our "young one"
from maturation.

With our eyes cast down
shoulders bent to the ground
we slump through our lives
victimized;
yet we can be victors
instead of victims
by choosing to walk in an upright position,
stitching closed the childhood incision,
a step that can only be our decision.

So let's lift up our heads
now is the hour
the past is past
it has no power
to guide the present
or control the future,
let go of its dead hand,
release it forever!

Pura Vida

Pura Vida—
the beautiful mantra of Costa Rica,
She waits like a mother for those who seek her,
fall on her lap, it's a place that's unique here...
where the weak grow strong
and the strong grow weaker...
She holds in her arms the world of the future
with army disarmed toward a culture of nurture
where the land is protected
and all beings respected.

Pura Vida—
Today I resolve to live a pure life
I can no longer handle personal scandal or strife.
I must be aligned with my authentic truth
to consistently live a life of true worth.
For me to be a positive influence
my head and my heart must join hands in
congruence.
When I'm facing temptation, depression, elation—
to dissolve the illusion, resolve the confusion
at the core of my being where sightlessly seeing
I ask only one question that transcends obsession
to make reality real:
How does this person,
action, situation—
make me really feel?

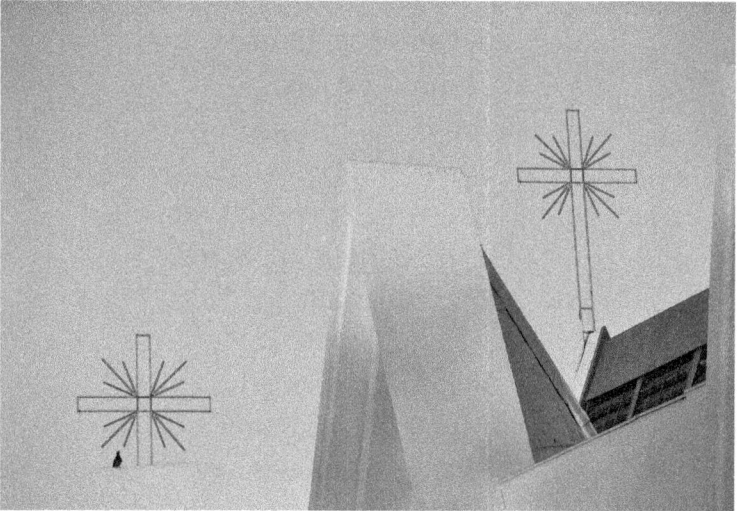

A Penny's Worth

A single penny
tossed in the trash
seemingly expendable
yet still spendable
miniscule cash;
Who can tell if it'll bring good luck?

Goodness knows it won't buy much.
Still, one hundred pennies
added up
equal a dollar
and that's enough
to fund the currency
of the government of
forever inked by the people's blood.

So what's a penny really worth?
It was minted on the fields of Gettysburg
a coin not perished from the Earth…

Venus Voyage

By the light of Venus
we crossed the open ocean,
rocked back and forth by rolling waves in motion
and no voodoo potion
or candles lit in devotion
could guarantee safe passage—
that much was certain,
especially in a boat so weathered and wooden.

At the helm in the stern
steered a fearless young Haitian
silhouetted at the bow
stood his mast-like companion.
I remarked to my son though I couldn't see him,
"This isn't *Pirates of the Caribbean*."

Suddenly, the helmsman cut the engine
to ride the crest of the wave that was coming
angling toward the bow
just off starboard
menacing and foaming.

The spray stung our faces and the tarp we were
under
offered little protection from saltwater thunder
and I have to admit I began to wonder
if our Ile a Vache trip might be a fatal blunder.

But suddenly we were docked
and scrambled ashore
the sea was behind us, Les Cayes before,
and as we walked along, I said to my son,
"Weren't you surprised that we didn't capsize
and weren't you afraid that we might drown
that the wooden boat might sink and never be
found?

He shook his head and quietly said,
"When you're in a situation that's out of your
control
you just have to hold on and you have to let go."

Zombies

"We laugh at death,
ha ha"
they said,
walked out the door
already dead.

"How are you?"
"We're here," they replied,
they vomited words, all hollow-eyed:
they could not surrender the flag of their pride:
Their bodies were living
but their spirits had died.

Solo Soul

We're the only person we can ever change,
the solo soul to rearrange;
Transformation's innately a choice
and when we choose for another
we silence their voice.

So, let us listen
and them speak
so they can find the love they seek;
And when at last lost love is found,
we'll find we're walking common ground...

No Expectation

If we can start each day
with anticipation
without a thought of expectation,
we'll discover serendipity
intersecting synchronicity
and our lives will no longer
follow routine
the groundhog days
of deja-vu scenes
and we'll create the space to dream
and manifest its realization
at liberty
from the tyranny
of routine expectation.

Shoulder to Shoulder

If we condescend and patronize
it will never harmonize
with being a friend
for friendship means equality
a sharing of mutuality
and honoring individuality,
not looking up
or looking down
but eye to eye
and arms around.

It's the only way to treat one another
shoulder to shoulder
as sister and brother.

Letting Go

When leaping into space
don't hesitate,
Free-falling faith
opens the gate.

You'll never know
just what you've got
or what lies below
until you jump from the top
and let go
let go
let
go.

Helpless

There are people you simply cannot help,
whose minds are locked like a prison cell,
who blame everything on everyone else
convinced that they're living in a living hell.

They cannot see that they've created
the life they've lived, the one they've hated
and they always feel they alone are fated
to wallow in abject misery
because of their personal history.

If they could just see
that there's no glory
in rehashing the past, the same old story,
but rewrite a new one with a different ending,
they could experience a new beginning...

Boxes and Lines

Thinking outside the box
coloring outside the lines,
breaking all the locks—
creativity defined.

What if there were no box
and what if there were no lines?
Would we throw away our clocks,
disregarding time?

Maybe we need the box
and maybe we need the lines—
We'd never know how freedom rocks
with boundaries undefined...

Purely Midwest
(inspired by the film, "Nebraska")

He just believes what people tell him,
can't imagine anyone's really a villain;
why would they lie in the things they're telling?
He can't sense when someone's
moving in for the killing.
Some say he'll fall for anything
especially if it's told by a "pretty young thing"
or written on official looking pieces of paper,
won't bother checking the fine print later.
He's old school,
the old fool,
still believes in the Golden Rule,
not hip to the come-on,
an easy mark for anyone,
he's never used disingenuity

as part of his vocabulary,
gullible to the hustle,
he trusts without question,
won't entertain doubt by suggestion,
won't listen to reason,
just wants to believe them,
still lives in a world,
guaranteed by his word,
sealed with a handshake
over a beer or a milkshake.
Some say he's deranged
but he'll never change;
he'll always feel that he was born blessed.
He's old school,
that old fool—
purely Midwest.

The Solitary Pair

They walk the same streets
but they will never meet—
this solitary pair.

Their parallel lives have never intersected
for they were never protected
from the holocaust
of human despair:

As a toddler,
he witnessed a murder
and all of his life he's cowered;
in her life as a wife
she was beaten senseless
and so, defenseless,
lives in a castle
with the drawbridge never lowered.

This solitary pair walks the same street
it seems like forever
but never
together...

Angels Share

Angels share
because they care
not just for themselves
but also for others,
seeing everyone as sisters and brothers,
sharing a common humanity,
the bond of a one-blooded family.

All About Them

Isn't it surprising
and isn't it sad
how you can go
from hero to zero
from good to bad
in just an instant
with someone you've sincerely befriended
when they decide to suddenly end it
and you say, "Please, just wait a minute,"
but they make it clear
they're no longer in it
because they didn't get their way this time
you couldn't make their day,
in living up to their expectation,
so they turn their back in termination.

It's tempting to think that you have "sinned"
and you know there's no way to begin again
with clearer eyes you see with surprise
from friendship's beginning until its end
It's always and ever been all about them...

A Guidance Parental

Seems so easy to be judgmental,
to see black and white
as fundamental.

But such an approach seems detrimental
to the Guidance inside us
so elemental;
for we are spirit as well as mental
and this life is not ours—
it's just a rental,

To play well with others
relate to our lovers,
we need the hand of a Guidance Parental.

Lachrymose Vs. Comatose

I'd rather be lachrymose than comatose
any day of being.
When tears are falling I'm feeling,
but when my eyes are closed, I'm sleeping
and sleeping just perpetuates
a somnolent, soporific state
from which my soul needs freeing...

Save Your Pity

"I feel sorry for you—
you didn't give me what I want
and now we're through."

"Save your pity for your own pity pot
I won't wallow in the pit
of the pity you've brought."

Human Versions

From "out there" extroverts
to "in here" introverts
for those with vision
and those with aversion
don't think the opposite
constitutes perversion—
They're simply
a complementary
human version.
And there's more than room
for all of us
to ride the personality bus.

Blues to Bluegrass

I'm done singin' the blues
time to vocalize a brighter note
than the color of cigarette smoke
in songs of melancholy hues.

I've strummed enough minor chords
to fill the songbook of my life,
It's time to score a new belief,
erase the lyrics of discouraging words.

I want to fingerpick the banjo
kick up my heels and fiddle
speed up the rhythm, return to the middle,
silence the mouth harp of my anger.

There are times we need to sing the blues
but if we sing them all the time
we play the victim's role in rhyme,
musicians of a darkened muse...

Soul Purpose

Love is our soul purpose
Joy is our birthright
so why be mirthless?

And how can any one of us be worthless
even if we're naked and walking shirtless
and even if a demon would dare to curse us,
and a debtor will never reimburse us,
nothing and no one can ever hurt us...

Yes, love is our soul's sole purpose,
conscious conscience of the universe,
revealed on those days at our best or worst,
perspiring in our run from last to first,
hyperventilating though our lungs might burst,
feeding at the breasts that we need to nurse
riding in the rain in the family hearse
crying with the breath of our newborn birth
lowered at our death into Mother Earth...

Winter Soulstice
Dec. 21, 2012

Today marks the end of the Mayan Calendar,
will it answer the question of what are we here for?
Will it be just another winter solstice
or an epiphany for priest and priestess
in the uterine temple of maternal goddess?
Time will tell,
of course it will
and time's our greatest ally
and the enemy we all flee...

Will it be a day of reckoning
or an equinox of beckoning
to live life on a higher plane
of dimensional evolution
purifying pollution
giving instead of taking
cooperating instead of competing

loving instead of hating
blessing instead of beating
nurture instead of torture—
we can't be sure
but to live with intention
just might prevent our species' declension
into planetary depravity
as we look back to nativity
as the ultimate solution
from eternal retribution.

Time will tell,
of course it will
and time's our greatest ally
and the enemy we all flee...

Modern Soul Family

I've finally found a place to belong
where I can sing my singular song,
a place where I can contribute my part
to the universal cathedral
of the evolving heart,
a place for the old and a place for the young,
a place for women and a place for men,
a place to be brother, a place to be friend
a place to start all over again;
A place where I can be myself
and not pretend to be anyone else,
a thoroughly modern soul family
where I am accepted unconditionally
and I return the favor reciprocally,
a place for non-egotistical sharing
based on the principle of simply caring,
a church without walls
I'm no longer alone
in a place that can only be known as home...

Back to Center

The masks we wear
the charades we play
to keep pursuing Javerts at bay—
the fashion shows
designer clothes
haughty high-heeled strut down the runway—
the black-tie-tuxedo
parties where elite go,
protecting the vulnerable child within
who rarely surfaces to skin
till the consequential

TANTRUM!

We're always on audition
to cover inhibition.
We play the roles we've been assigned
no matter that we're misaligned,
playing our brothers and sisters
like vampiric shape shifters
until a warm and loving mentor
gently brings us back
to center...

Addiction Affliction

All addictions
medicate emotional afflictions,
anesthetizing the feelings
we don't want to feel,
perpetuating fantasy
disrupting our serenity,
repressing the real.

And the only way we can ever heal
is to simply stop drugging
and feel what we feel,
letting layer by layer
slowly unpeel.
until authenticity
is fully revealed.

But if we never let ourselves feel what we feel,
if we lie to ourselves and always conceal,
our addictions will continue to rape and to steal
every beautiful dream
and finally kill...

FaceLook

All we want is to be liked,
to be acknowledged,
and recognized
as having value and worth
in others' eyes.

But the more we reach
for that unreachable prize
we begin to realize
that the face looking back at us
in the reflection
of the bathroom glass
is the only face we can always trust,
the one who really loves us the most
and when the last post
of a friend has ended
we can never be unfriended...

Presents of Presence

No diamond ring
glittering with bling
or gilded offering
of anything
can bring
joy to share
like being there—
aware and listening.
This is the essence of giving presents:
the quintessential gift of our presence...

The Wannabe Daddy

The count was full when Daddy pitched the ball;
The little boy swung but he cleanly whiffed,
"Strike Three!" was the call as he fell to the ground
corkscrewed like a licorice twist.
Daddy stood there with his hands on his hips,
a boys-of-summer smile playing on his lips.
He saw the small hand— the bat still in its grip
as he pounded his fist into the pocket of his mitt.
He decided to ask his boy a question,
not at all to teach him a lesson,
but simply for his own information.
"So when you grow up, what do you want to be?"
He asked the question casually.
The boy stood up and grinned impishly.
"You wanna know what I wanna be?
That's easy!
I wanna be a daddy!"

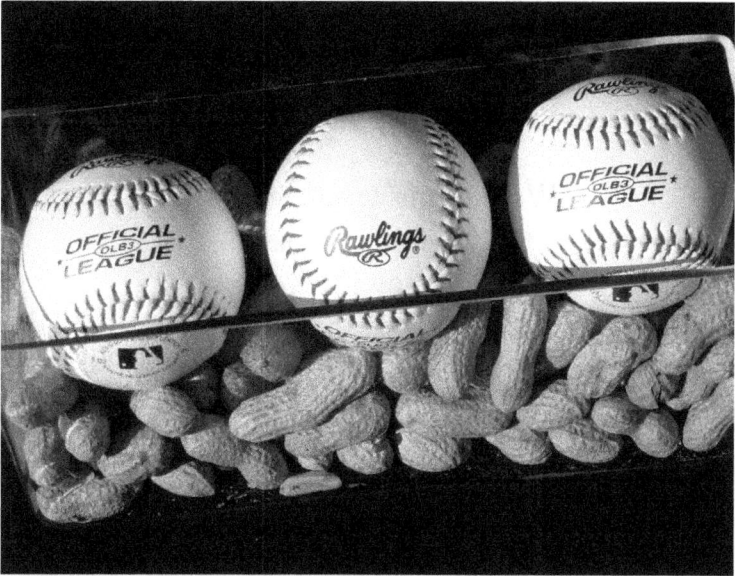

Focus the Fire!

"If we want to make a fire, we have to focus all the sun's rays on one spot. And the great secret that the Divine Energy revealed to the world was fire. And there comes a moment when we need to focus that inner fire so that our life will have some meaning."
~Paulo Coelho, Manuscript Found in Accra, page 67

With incendiary desire,
I focus my inner fire,
igniting a conflagration—
not the flaring flames of a funeral pyre
but a bonfire of illumination,

Welcoming young and old
to come out of the cold
to a place they feel protected,
where they can warm their shivering souls
and never feel neglected.

A fire that we can dance around
sing songs of celebration,
a love party thrown for everyone
without discrimination.

And when my fire is smoldering low
and ashes form from glowing coals,
I'll touch a torch to a single spark
and pass it on to light the dark.

There comes a time in every life
when power must be relinquished,
yet the fire will burn eternally
and never be extinguished.

A Dietary Declaration of Independence

I'm so so done with structured plans,
powders and pills.
Today I'm writing my own dietary rules
based on how a meal
makes my body feel...

I won't abide by the dictates of dietary gurus,
whether animal-protective vegans
or omnivorous paleos.

Within reason
I'll eat in season:
when it's cold, soups and stews
will warm my soul.

I probably won't eat watermelon when the ground
is frozen,
or have Thanksgiving Dinner
in the middle of the summer.
When I'm feeling heated
a cool refreshing salad will be just what's needed.

Though I know fresh is best,
I won't go to WAR over going RAW
or worry about the advantage of a particular
percentage.

Detoxification is not my emancipation.
For me, it's hypoglycemic starvation
turning into a ravenous orgy—
eating whatever the fridge sets before me...

Everything lives by eating what's available,
the huntress said in the *Poisonwood Bible,*
which simply means everything's edible
but not everything's necessarily digestible.

My dietary rules have come to fruition
through the nutritive power of intuition,
the individualized science of nutrition.

But my diet book collection chronicles restriction:
eat specific foods in certain combinations,
and for goodness sake you must avoid gluten!

And you'd better wean yourself from dairy—
because to nature, it's contrary.
I will admit, GMOs are scary
and Monsanto just might be
the evil food fairy.

But I'll give props to Ben and Jerry's
because I love ice cream
and not soy or coconut
but baby, the real thing!
not every day, please understand, but once in a
while—
there's nothing sweeter to make me smile
on a summer day when it's hot and steamy,
the taste of it's so cool and creamy.

I just can't be obsessed
because some foods are processed
or become pedantic about always eating organic
or even stridently vocal about foods local,
because it's not always affordable or convenient,
so I'm learning to be more lenient,
doing the best that I can
following a flexible dietary plan—
I've found it to be the best way of eating
at the banquet table of dietary freedom!

Emoceanal

Feelings ebb
Feelings flow,
life is so *emoceanal.*

Ever conscious of the tide
we set the compass of our lives,
then a thought without anchor
drifts from the harbor
to the open sea
of white-capped danger,
embarking on a *knotical* adventure
to test in weather
the seaworthy sailor.

Yes and No

Be careful to what you say yes to;
an affirmative carries the implication
of long-term, maybe even lifetime, obligation
and potentially complicated extrication.

Be aware of what you say no to;
a reply in the negative
is certainly your prerogative
but it might close the door
to opportunity and initiative.

You don't need to consult a Ouija board
or even flip over a Tarot card.
Just learn to listen to your Intuition,
the voice inside you that's there to guide you
to the correct response
with no regrets of woebegone...

Every Lone Ranger

Every lone ranger needs a partner,
a Tonto to share the next adventure,
a silver bullet to fire for justice,
a horse named Silver to ride into the distance...

No ranger can be a solo crusader,
a white-hat, black-mask masquerader;
you need someone to ride beside you,
track the trail and always guide you.

They may not look at all like you
or speak the language that you do,
call you Kemo Sabe in Comanche tongue,
but listen to their counsel for they're rarely wrong.

Every lone ranger facing danger
is sometimes thrown into the biggest puddle,
but faithful Tonto promptly picks you up
and lifts you right back into the saddle.
Yes, faithful Tonto promptly picks you up
and lifts you right back into the saddle...

Just Be

Be mindful
be grateful
not unkind
and never hateful.

Be humble
be useful
never ruthless
or untruthful.

Be authentic
be real
never false
or artificial.

Be now
be here
not then
or over there.

Be innocent
be elastic
never rigid
or sarcastic.

Be you
be free
not them
and never me.

Be polite
be dignified
never rude
or preoccupied.

Be gentle
be understanding
never strident
or demanding.

Be sensual
but also gracious
never pandering
or salacious.

It's a simple philosophy:
Just be
just
be
be...

Mirror Mirror

The beauty I see in you
mirrors the beauty I see in me;
The ugliness you see in you
reflects the ugliness you see in me...

Are there any other images
we could possibly see
in the reflective windows
of shared humanity?

Mirror Mirror on the wall,
there is no fairest of us all,
neither cause for triumph
nor for jealousy...

Beautiful Selves

Just be your beautiful self
and I'll be mine;
Why even think of trading places?
We'd be misaligned.
I wouldn't be able to move your body;
You'd be hard pressed to think with my mind.

Don't see us paired as repulsive polarity
but partnered together
with magnetic complementarity.

You were born
to inhabit a certain form,
one I cannot duplicate;
and far from doing any harm
our different norm
is something we can celebrate.

In Spirit, we indeed, may be one,
but here on Earth from the moment of birth,
we must learn to live together alone;
It all comes down to others
and how we consistently treat them.
This temporary separation
guarantees our freedom
while solidifying our union...

In Sync

It was what it was,
it is what it is,
it will be what it will be.
We can only do so much
to alter history.

Our only viable option
is to choose our own reaction
to every single incident,
no accident, coincidence—
just synchronicity...

Separatione

Here I am
and there's you,
are we one or are we two?
The pendulum swings
on point of view.

If we merely consider
ego and form,
then separation
is clearly born,
the undeniable cultural norm.

But if instead we're speaking of essence,
the formlessness of conscious presence,
then gender and age,
profession and place,
and culture and race
present a masqueraded face,
and when at last the masks are trashed,
awareness dissolves illusion:
There never was and never is
any real division.

The Road Home

When we're fully aligned
with our souls,
the pathway of life
just naturally unfolds,
leading us on to a yellow brick road ,
to emerald cities,
and treasures of gold
with fields of poppies along the way
where we can rest at the end of the day,
alongside our trusted traveling companions:
tin men, scarecrows and cowardly lions,
we help them obtain the gifts that they seek—
a brain, a heart and courage complete.
And when our journey's finally done,
all of us can go back home,
where love alone occupies the throne...

The Missing I

Life is merely theory
until we experence
the birth of a daughter
or death of a father,
earn a diploma,
battle lymphoma—

It doesn't become real
until we can feel
the kiss of a lover,
embrace of a mother,
pain of separation,
righteous indignation.

One little letter underscores variance
from the word of experience
it's the same little letter for pride:

We can't know the ocean
until we've sailed it ourselves
and the waves beach our boat
with the tide...

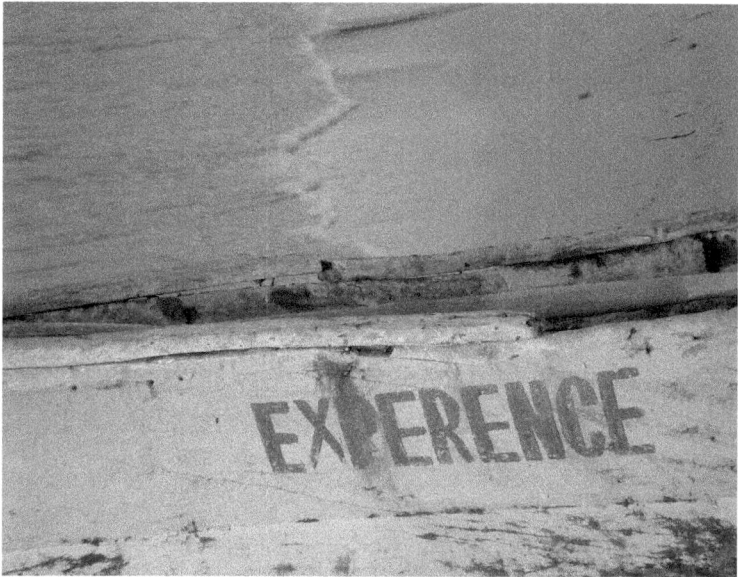

Primary Care

I don't care what you think about me
if you don't care what you think about you,
because you can't care about anyone,
the highs and the lows they're going through.

Only when we care first for ourselves,
are we able to care about anyone else.
It seems so very elementary
this managed care
primal, primary.

Beyond Betrayal

The greatest betrayal
is the betrayal of ourselves:
Always living to please everyone else
turns us into our very own Judases,
blaming others for our abuses
then making excuses for our behavior
and looking for a savior
to bear the cross for us.
But maybe for once instead of salvation,
we all just need gentle affirmation:
We might just be okay with our scars and flaws:
The mind always lies
but the body never does...

The Consequential Boomerang

We have the freedom to say what we want,
autonomous power to praise or to taunt,
but every word spoken with whatever intent
carries the weight of consequence.
And we all must pay that linguistic price—
vindictive and mean
or loving and kind;
It all comes back to us in hand,
spit at foe or whispered to friend:
the consequential boomerang.

The Opposite Effect

If there were no death,
we'd take life for granted,
If there were no pain,
growth would ever be stunted.

If there were no hate,
we wouldn't know how to love,
If there were no below,
we'd never look above.

If there were no aging,
we'd always be young,
we'd forever be right,
never admit when we're wrong.

If there were no loss,
there would be no gain,
we'd have more than enough,
yet always complain.

If there were no dark,
we couldn't see the light,
If there were no wrong,
we wouldn't know what's right.

If there were no cold,
we'd never seek warmth,
and gather together
around the heat of the hearth.

If there were no man,
there would be no woman,
If there were no woman,
would we even be human?

If there were no war,
would we truly know peace?
We'd have nothing to forgive
and forever release.

If there were no sickness,
would we appreciate health?
If there were no poverty,
would we invest in wealth?

If there were no hunger,
we'd always be full,
we wouldn't know the emptiness
of the beggar's bowl.

If there were no chaos,
there wouldn't be order,
no puzzle to put back
carefully together.

There must be a reason
opposites attract
and why they elicit
the opposite effect.

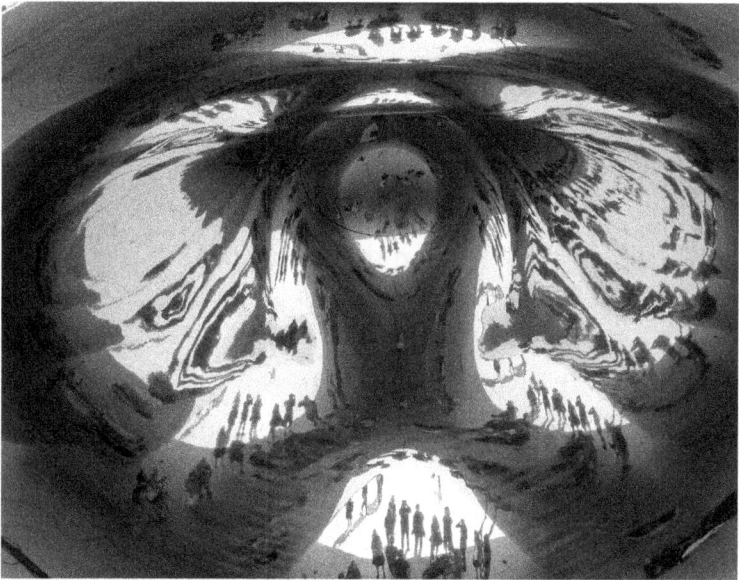

Between the Lines of Inner Lives

How little we know
of those who go,
and when they're gone
the mystery lives on.

Their history hides between the lines
and we can only speculate
in reading obit, Facebook page,
the introspective, personal trajectory
of their inner lives...

Embracing the Attraction

It's healthier to embrace the attraction
and express my deepest heartfelt affection
in a manner appropriate to the situation,
than to deny my feelings and repress my longings,
which only sharpens the hunger for belonging
toward the ravenous direction
of inappropriate boundary crossings...

You are the gift...

You are the gift
the world's been waiting for,
the one no one can buy
at the big box store,
or order online with free shipping and more—
discount coupons,
calculated score...
And not only the gift,
but the giver as well—
you may not think you have something to tell,
but search your heart and you will definitely see
unlimited potentiality.
The things that come so easy for you,
the ones impossible for others to do
are the very things they can only get from you.

They're yours by Divine inheritance
but require daily maintenance
and lifelong diligence,
and they're not dependent
on measured intelligence.
You get what you pay for
is an old adage but true,
so the question is
what will you do?
Will you hoard it or hide it,
give it away to be "nice"
or charge what you're worth,
a pearl of great price?

Genomology

Flesh and blood
and bone alone
can't chart the graph
of our own genome.
Double Helix DNA
we may be,
but we are more
than chemistry
determined genetically.
For we are royalty
descended from another realm,
trying to find our way
back home...

Island Life

Earth orbits as island
in sea of space;
conditions for life
exist
in one remarkable place—
the Big Blue Marble with a human face.

And from here
where could we really go
to live
in the planetary archipelago?

Mercury's too hot,
Pluto's too cold,
but Earth is just right
for the life that we hold.

Graced with water
warmed by the sun,
in the solar system,
the singular one.

Intelligent life exists in the universe—
it's crazy, but maybe
only on planet Earth.
And maybe it's that way by Divine design,
that intelligent life has been confined
to one orbital island
so we can find
the way to live and love

and mutually thrive,
stop fighting each other
in wars of mass suicide.

If we don't, it's certain we will all pay the price,
as our island erodes
into *Lord of the Flies*.

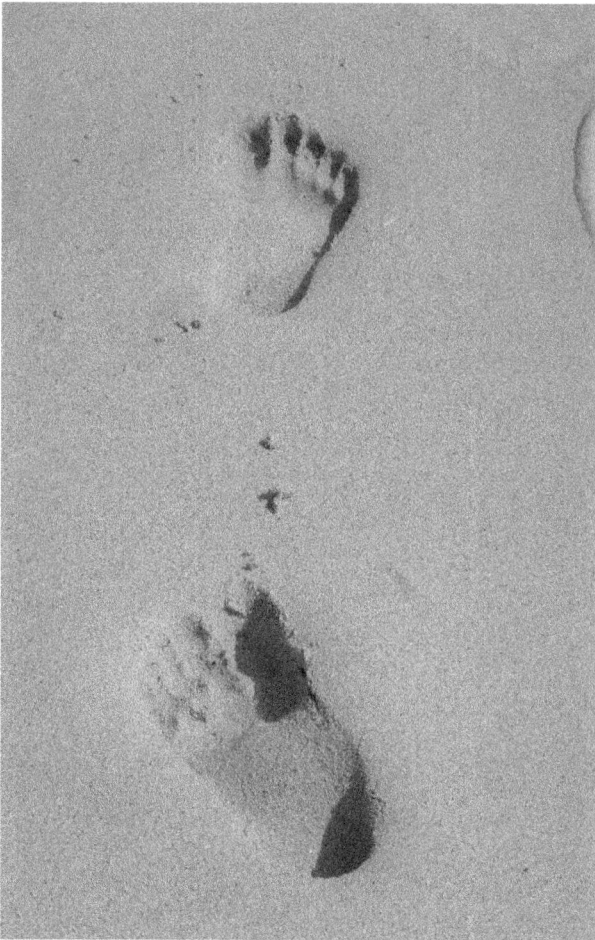

Blessing and Curse

Just when we think things couldn't get worse,
when we seem to be driving in reverse,
it's helpful to remember,
with unconditional surrender,
there's a curse in every blessing
and a blessing in every curse.

Their Undoing

"You can't do enough for me," she said.
"You don't do it for me anymore," he replied.
Their relationship was unraveling,
a cord no longer unified.

They were beginning to comprehend
their relationship was nearing end,
a page that could not be refreshed
until she did it for herself,
and he did it for himself as well,
and then, and only then
could their relationship begin again:
a focus on renewing,
reversal of undoing,
reestablishment as friends.

Life Offline

I don't want to live my life online;
I've got better things to do with my time
than mindlessly surfing cyberspace,
scrolling and trolling my Facebook page,
sharing all my interests on Pinterest,
tweeting things that don't really matter,
frittering away my time on Twitter.

I remember the time when no one was online
and we didn't feel deprived
or any less alive.
We played football after school before supper at
night,
no fantasy football to fantasize
or a web cam skyping in our eyes.
Now everyone's fingering their smart phones
with texts coming in like unmanned drones
no one knows how to be alone...

Is anyone anymore paying attention;
is anyone present and really listening?
Would anyone suddenly become dumb
if they didn't have a smart phone to thumb?

I don't want a relationship
with artificial intelligence
even if HER voice is Scarlett Johansen's,
a voice that sets every man's hormones dancing.
And I prefer a book I can hold in my hand
instead of Nook or Kindle inscribed in sand.

Don't get me wrong, online has its place,
but I don't want my life
to be a virtual waste.
I don't want to live with my mind in the Cloud;
I want to be able to laugh out loud.
I simply want to live in a world that's real
with what I can touch, taste and feel,
because only the tangible
makes the world intelligible...
and truly enjoyable.

Happily Ever After

At the next table,
two little girls
wiggled and giggled,
fluffed their princess dresses,
smoothed their carefully coiffed tresses,
stuffed their pretty little faces,
not exactly delicate.
They were learning tea room etiquette
while their doting mothers
posed them together—
a photo for posting
on Facebook later.

And later that day
for the matinee,
would they see Belle in *Beauty*
or Clara in *The Nutcracker*?
It's doubtful to them it really mattered
for this moment they were laughing together
and much later in life they would remember
this day of happily ever after.

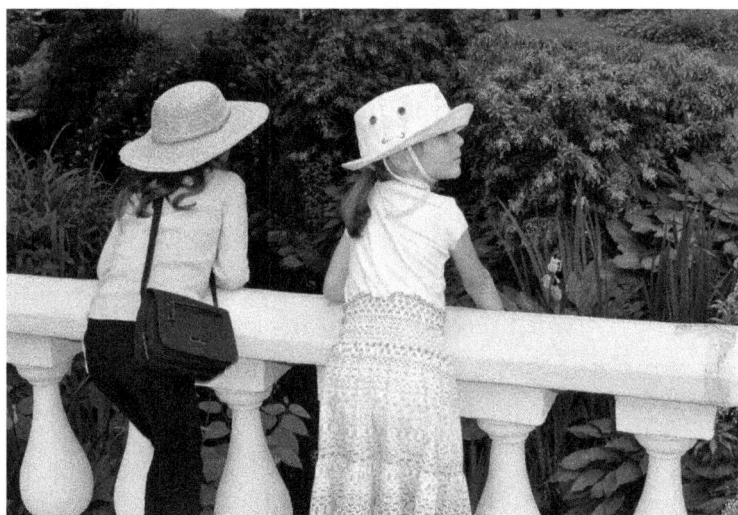

Reds

It was formal night
and she was standing at the bar
at eye level
in scarlet stilettos,
a martini or two had made her feel mellow,
and in her hair,
tilted there
she wore a crimson fascinator,
and she was fascinated
by my red bow tie and red beret
and it prompted her to say,
"Could we take a photo together,
a picture to preserve this moment forever?"
And I said, "Of course."
There's nothing worse
than refusing a young lady
with a matching purse…
and besides, by my side
stood my wife,
who without hesitation
embraced the momentary fascination,
our transgenerational color coordination.

So we stood together side by side,
dressed to the nines with mutual pride,
our arms tentatively around each other,
waiting for the click of the camera's shutter.

But the very next day,
as we passed each other in the passageway,
magical formalities reverted to realities.
I glanced in her eyes,
but she didn't acknowledge or recognize
who we were the night before
in the threads of red that we wore.
Nothing is ever and could be normal
on a night on the ship designated formal.

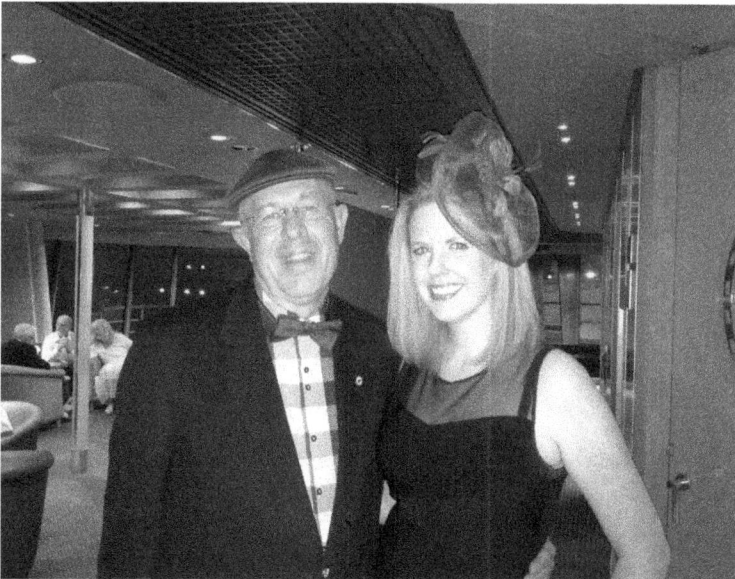

Photo by Connie Saxton

The Ultimate O

Letting go,
the Ultimate O,
waves of pleasure
break on the beach of your soul.
It begins with a smile
then morphs into laughter—
lights up everything that's solemnly dark here,
and you won't want to smoke a cigarette after...
You don't need to take off your clothes
or swing at an orgy,
get tied up by "Christian"
in shades-of-gray quirky.
You just have to share the blessing of humor
and you simply start by a look in the mirror.
Can you see the natural-born comic
reflected there for others to mimic?
You can share it with everyone.
You don't need a partner
and you don't have to play
a game of solitaire,
be acrobatic

or use prophylactic;
you don't need protection
when your heart shines affection.

Just be spontaneous
and it will be simultaneous,
and if you're especially affable,
it will definitely be multiple.
If you want to know what you're truly worth,
share the gift of your innocent mirth.
We all must face reality
but comedy trumps tragedy
and levity
is lighter than gravity.
If you are divided and want to be whole,
just laugh, laugh, laugh and let yourself go.
Feel it now, the Ultimate O—
euphoric, transcendent
orgasm of the soul...

Darkness and Light

We're all angels
and we're all demons
and the being we become
is the spirit we are feeding,
the one of darkness or light.
It's a matter of choosing
who's winning or losing
and whether our wings take flight
or remain forever folded
in the shadows of the night.

More than Enough

Now comes the day of the driveway auction,
when hoarded treasures sell for a fraction;
The cadence of the auctioneer—
plays music to the bidder's ear:

Now three, now three,
who'll give me four?
Who'll give me five—
it's worth much more!

To those who are selling,
his singsong sounds like yelling,
a voice they'd rather never hear:

Now six, now six
and now it's seven—
sold to the lady with number eleven!

Why is it so hard to give up stuff
that sits on our shelves gathering dust
or in the garage collecting rust,
when we have more
than more than enough?

Robes of Androgyny

Why does God have to be a he,
a patriarchal trinity?

Couldn't God just as well be a she,
the mother of humanity?
Even Jesus emerged from a womb
and when He rose from the darkened tomb,

Mary was first (not his mother)
to greet Him as a spiritual lover;
she was there alone without his brothers.
So, does God wear a mantle of misogyny,
or could it be that Divinity
is clothed in the robes of androgyny?

Rite to Life

The last time I saw you
you were celebrating ten years of marriage
and you looked me in the eye.

This time you were pushing a baby carriage
and you made sure to glance away.
I was surprised to learn of your separation
and the child wasn't the baby of your first husband.
I can't help but wonder
just what happened?

You were always the virtuous one,
the joyful unflappable Christian.
But was that just a porcelain mask,
Was the role you were playing
too much to ask?
Somehow, Ariel,
you cracked.

Was it you,
was it him,
was it an affair unplanned
when things one night
got out of hand?

You were the one who never wanted children
because of the world's overpopulation.
But maybe one night's indiscretion
permanently changed
your maternal position.

I'll never know
because you'll never tell
and we really never knew
each other that well.

I'd rather just leave things as they are,
respecting each other's space from afar.
It's certainly not my place to judge;
All I can do from a distance is love
and admire your choice to do what's right
as you walk the passage of rite to life...

Relationship Reciprocity

A healthy relationship is reciprocal,
giving and taking in measures equal,
supporting each other in interdependence,
an unbreakable bond when the world is against us
and when one or the other
feels down or defenseless,
yet a flexible band that welcomes friendship
to the sacred circle of partnership
and allowing each other a measure of freedom
even in times when we feel we most need them.

It is this balance,
this homeostasis,
that sustains the healthiest
of human relationships.

No Diploma

Life is a school
from which we never graduate—
Its learning curve's the steepest grade —
we can just matriculate.

And though we'll never march across
the stage in cap and gown,
the curriculum we've chosen
is uniquely just our own.

Just when we think we've learned enough
to finally go on in,
the revolving door of education
turns us back again.

Fine Wine

It's certainly wisdom
to carefully listen
and consider others' advice,
but if you're inclined
to do it all the time
just to be nice,
you'll water down the flavor
of your own fine wine.

And what a waste
that no one will pay
to uncork the bottle
and savor the taste
of your undeniable,
single varietal,
uniquely complex bouquet.

Now and Know

We can be in the now
but not be in the know
if we've never learned how
to say yes and no,
answers essential
for potential to grow.

And we can be in the know
but not be in the now,
disregarding the flow,
the shot across the bow.

It's only when we know
and also live in the now,
that we can ever go
and grace the higher place of Tao.

Emily and Justin

Her name was Emily,
a Jewish young woman from the Borough of
Brooklyn;
Her boyfriend, Justin, hailed from Manhattan.
Emily was learning to teach meditation
Justin, an attorney for a real estate corporation—

Both were native New Yorkers,
that rarest of rare domiciliary combinations.
They met at a concert and their life's syncopation
segued into soul mate collaboration.
Now they cook breakfast together
and drink only fair trade beverages,
unconcerned with the fluctuating Dow Jones
Average.
They came to Costa Rica seeking peace and
freedom
and on the sunset cruise we were destined to meet
them.
We talked about nutrition,
and Emily, the daughter of a pediatrician,
said she believed in the power of intuition
and I said, "What about synchronicity?"
Her brown eyes brightened at the possibility
as a shimmering dolphin arced skyward
out of the Caribbean sea.

Justin still wears suits to his office on a daily basis
but he's seeking the peace of a different oasis
after reading a book called "The Greedy Bastards."

Emily dresses down in slippers and leotards,
a therapist who heals with the gentlest touch,
she's marrying her hands with positive thought.

We knew this magical voyage couldn't last
as the sun set in the west
and the moon rose in the east,
framed by the sail and the perpendicular mast.

We wished for each other abundance and blessing
and I paused a moment in silent reflection
as I considered this cruise and a one-time
connection
with the beautiful Emily
and her boyfriend, Justin.

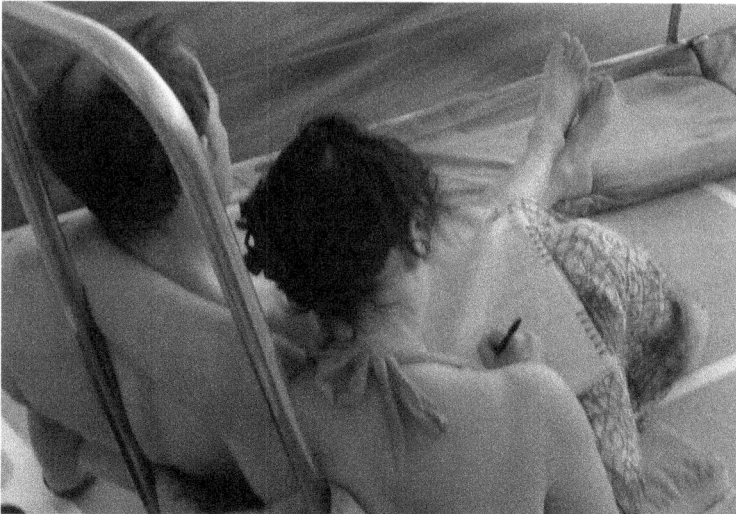

Powerbill

If you won the Powerball,
the whole shebang,
the sum of it all,
what would you do with all that money,
the millions in the pot
of the Powerball Lottery?

Would you spend it profligately
on cars, boats and gadgetry?
Would you travel around the world
collecting diamonds, emeralds and pearls,
flying first class from nation to nation
luxuriating on permanent vacation?

Would family and friends you hadn't seen in a long
time
suddenly show up
with you on their minds?
And if you didn't share the wealth,
would they simply dismiss
your miserly self?

Maybe you'd give away most for free
to your favorite charity,
keeping just enough of the rest
for a rainy day
and to feather your nest.

Or would you invest it like Warren Buffet,
turning millions to billions
in fiduciary profit,
using it for philanthropy,
setting up a foundation
in perpetuity?

At any rate, you know there'd be tax,
the government would take its half;
before you'd ever endorse that check,
the IRS would show up to collect.

And at the end of the day,
you couldn't take it with you anyway.
If you won the Powerball,
the whole shebang, the sum of it all,
there'd be a Powerbill to pay.

Sister(s)

Yellowstone Park was your last known destination;
you were returning home to California
from vacation
when your body was burned
beyond recognition.

They shipped your ashes home in an urn;
little Kelly cradled it in her arms
as if to protect you from further harm.

You were my one and only sister;
I was your one and only brother.
We grew up together in suburban Denver.

All of these years I have missed you,
but you should know I've been blessed too
by the sisters I've been introduced to,
soul sisters, in fact, who share my vision
of loving all people without possession,
and I know that too
was your singular passion.

You, the homebody, embodied the best;
I still feel the touch of your caring caress,
mother and sister and friend at rest.

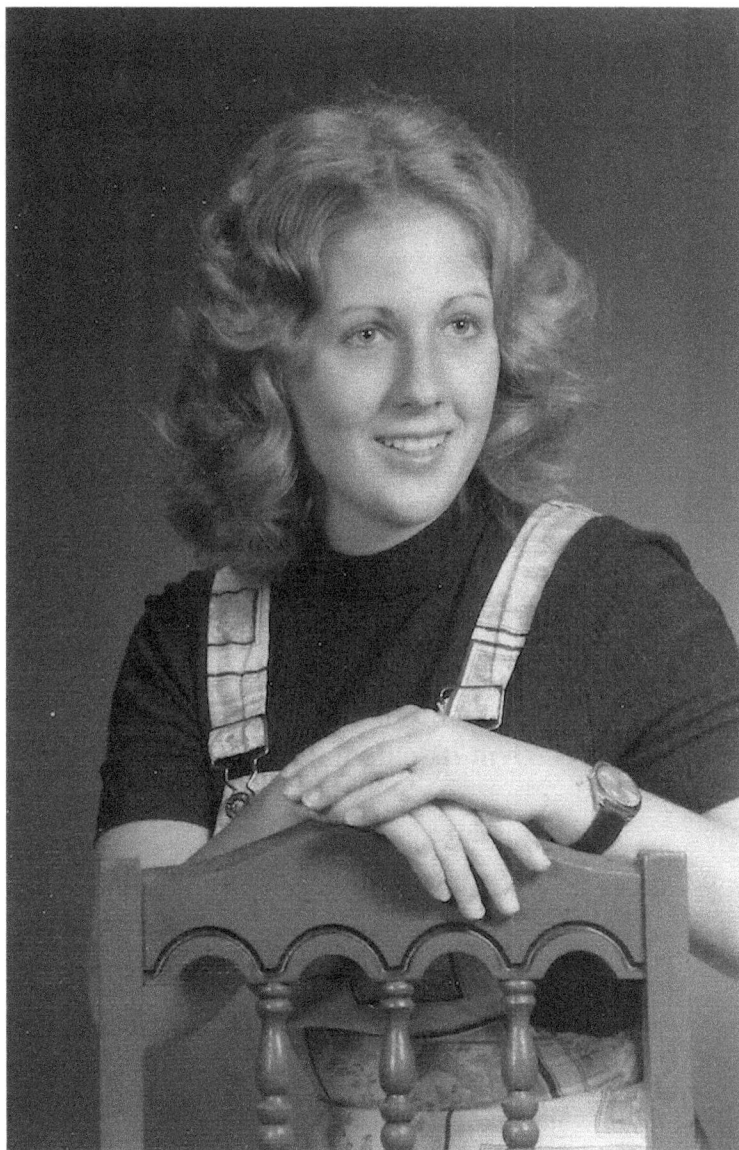

In Loving Memory
Patty Kay Fly Dittmar, 6/9/58 – 7/14/89

Decimal

A decimal
might seem infinitesimal,
but that tiny little dot,
that barely perceptible spot
placed in the equation
makes all the difference
in its calculation.

Section 3

Nature

Elegy for Snowflake

Winter saddled Snowflake in the middle of
summer;
an alabaster mare,
no one ever rode her.
She just nibbled grass peacefully in the pasture
and the seasons segued seamlessly
one into another,
until the July morning when her devoted owners,
Herb and Betty Wampler,
found her lying on her side,
eyes wide with pain and fear.

They called the vet who simply said,
"It's colic and I could haul her to the clinic.
An operation is the only chance
we have right now to save her."
Herb scratched his head, thought long and hard,
looked at Betty—who'd let down her guard.
"Just put her down, that's the only thing that's fair.
We can't afford the operation
even though we love her.
And there's no guarantee, is there, Doc,
that Snowflake would get better?"

Now Snowflake is buried in the very ground that
fed her,
the Northwest Missouri acre
she fertilized with her own manure.

As for me, I will always miss her;
in the season of the clover and the thistle,
Snowflake would come trotting
at the sound of my whistle.
She would shake her mane,
I'd extend my hand
and feed her crunchy apples,
and the juice would always dribble
from her soft and whiskered lips
in sweet and sticky trickles...

Evergreen

May we ever be
evergreen
seen the same
in the changing scene
branches bow
under weight of snow
still
evergreen
in moonlight glow.

And when summer comes
in burst of flame
still
evergreen
in the quenching rain.

Seasons come, seasons go
sometimes fast, sometimes slow
we remain the same as the seasons change
in winter snow
or summer rain
forever and ever

evergreen...

All Snow

We're all unique
our very own snowflake
We don't repeat
our crystallized makeup.

Not one of us can claim
to be patterned the same
even though
we're all just snow.

Autumnal

All of a sudden
everything seems autumnal.
The cicadas are singing
from September's hymnal;
the sun shines mellower
on my shoulder
and I'm feeling older
than I can remember...

But it's more than okay
to feel that way,
to carry a lighter load
than sizzling in summer
like a firecracker fuse
waiting to explode.

So, I will relax in this autumn time
and gather the harvest of my life,
let the leaves of my tree
tumble one by one
down to the ground
in the brisk October breeze
until at last
they're covered by the frost
of the first November freeze...

Tree Light

Trees always reach for the light
and the sturdiest grow in groves
nourished by fallen branches past,
the leaves of the decomposed.
Trees always reach for the light
by rain and wind opposed,
the elemental forces
that force all trees to grow.
Trees always reach for the light;
a seedling to sapling knows
photosynthesis is the antithesis
to how hard the north wind blows...

Bird of Pray

I am an eagle
winging solo
over crag and peak
where no flocks go...
but I'm not solitary
in the aerie
I mate for life-
nesting is my avian truth.

With telescopic eye
and echoing scream,
I see the planetary dream:
Everything is interconnected,
nothing and no one to be rejected,
though vulnerable eaglets must be protected...

As for me
I am a raptor free
rising higher and higher
every day—
aerodynamic bird of pray.

Ten Thousand Apples

Ten Thousand Apples
ripened on the tree,
a harvest so great
that Gregory
felt compelled to count them
and give them for free,
a modern-day
Johnny Appleseed.

"To let them rot on the ground
would be a waste;
I made some applesauce
would you like a taste?
The apples are natural,
not tainted with poison.
Would you like a bag,
maybe a dozen?"

And then Gregory said something
simply profound
about ten thousand apples
tumbling down:
"I just couldn't let them rot on the ground
The apples on my apple tree
belong as much to you
as they do to me."

Section 4

Current Events

The Invisible Sword

They say the pen is mightier than the sword,
and who can deny the power of the word?
Just ask those who heard Lincoln
at Gettysburg...
or Martin Luther King
and his "I have a dream..."

The Strongest Spoke

Livestrong Lance finally admitted
he used drugs to win it,
The Tour De France
not just once but seven times over,
a competitive conspiracy so undercover—
the recycling odyssey of a cancer survivor
and compulsive liar.

He opened up to Oprah, his first mea culpa.
After years of denial and threat of a trial,
stripped of his medals,
he continued the guile,
his laser beam eyes
betrayed the hint of a smile...

But overwhelming evidence
weakened resistance
until helmetless, the spokeless spokesman
finally admitted,
yes,
he used drugs to win it.
And as an enforcement,
Nike cancelled his contract endorsement—
But they couldn't just do it
until they knew he did it.

The last will be first and the first will be last,
the future will come, erasing the past,
the pedals will stop their circular motion
and the roadside fans will cease their devotion,

the bicycle chains will oxidize to rust
and the phalanx of riders disintegrate to dust.

So, is there a moral to Armstrong's story?
It may well be life's cruelest joke—
cycling for trophies and podium glory
with an unconscious conscience
bends the strongest spoke...

Gun Control, Mayberry Style

Andy only used a gun when he had to,
but most of the time he didn't,
resolving Mayberry's conflicts
with calmness and intelligence.

Barney couldn't be trusted with one;
his single issued bullet
was buttoned up safely
in his front shirt pocket.

Maybe it's time for a personal background check:
even-tempered or nervous wreck?
Just who are we—
an open-collared sheriff
or a tight-tied deputy?

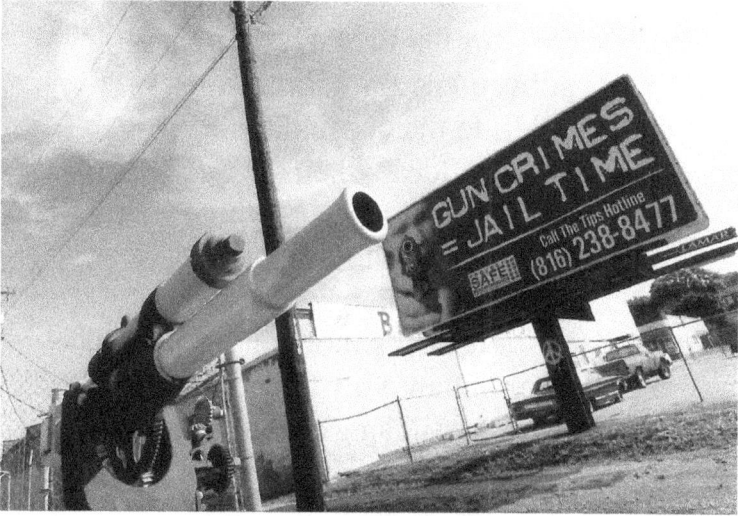

Marrowthon

A double explosion at the finish line,
the siren scream
and frightened stampede,
runners oblivious of place and time.
Limbs amputated,
families devastated,
victims of the Brothers Tsarnaev
never even knew what they died of,
that was left to the conscious survivors—
and the first responders when they arrived there.

Makeshift tourniquets
tied around bleeding stumps,
a dancer's foot gone
and her valiant vow to dance on...
Adrianna's still singing her song—
she's Boston strong.

Instant heroes,
Good Samaritan Jane and John Does,
yet three dorm mates, in spite of consequence,
conspired to conceal incriminating evidence.
And what about Tamerlan's wife, the American?
Was she a silent accessory assassin
or just another brainwashed victim
of her domineering and extremist husband?
Where was her attention
when the bombs were assembled in the kitchen?

Flags at half mast,
casualties blessed—
Chechen Brothers,
jihadist bombers,
killing the infidel,
creating a living hell.
Do jehovahs, krishnas and allahs
demand violence of their followers
to smell the incense of sulfurous intolerance?

Dzhokhar's note, scribbled in the boat,
spoke to the motive the attack provoked:
the casualties were merely collateral damage;
never mind the fact they were made in God's
image
or at the very least had a human visage.

A failure to assimilate
fertilized the seeds of hate.
Tamerlan said, "Those Americans,
I just don't understand them—
I claim none of them as my friends;
they bombed Iraq and Afghanistan,
we'll bomb the Boston Marathon!"
The amateur pugilist
could not win with his fists—
Downloading files of Al Qaeda's *Inspire*
lit the fuse,
ignited the fire.

The Russians warned the CIA
who alerted the FBI,

but somehow both agencies
struggling internally,
turned a blind and bureaucratic eye.

A video surveillance camera
identified the perpetrators,
but they would not be amenable
to negotiators...

A city on lockdown,
the carjacking, gunfight and knockdown,
the hovering helicopter,
the sudden SWAT team capture,
the continuing investigation,
Bostonian celebration.

Back on Boylston Street,
empty now of runners' feet—
Three dead and thirteen amputees,
memorial display of bouquets and wreaths—
business not as usual,
life not as casual...

And then at the end of the season,
triumph beyond reason—
The World Series Trophy,
Red Sox Glory.
At the place of the bomb,
they broke into song,
617—Boston Strong...

All hearts turned toward Boston,

with empathetic compassion
for we had lost with them.
We felt it in our deepest marrow,
dazed and confused,
incomprehensible sorrow,
facing our own uncertain tomorrow...

But improvised acts of senseless violence
fueled by hate can never silence
intentional ones of genuine kindness,
for love alone defuses
bombs of blindness,
clearing the way for us to break
the evolutionary tape
and finally cross the finish line
of our collective marathon.

Foreign Born

I ask myself the question
again and again,
if I had been born in a foreign land,
let's just say, Afghanistan,
or maybe Saudi Arabia,
would I have joined the Taliban
or Osama Bin Laden's Al Quaeda?

Would I have become a desperate and irate
gaunt-cheeked, hollow-eyed Somali pirate
hijacking commercial freighters
in international waters,
holding the captain for millions in ransom,
or invade a Kenyan mall
as one of Al Shabab's infidel haters?

Or born here as an immigrant,
culturally tied to a different continent
and facing an identity crisis;
would I radicalize
and fight for ISIS?

I'd like to think I wouldn't,
but maybe I just couldn't
escape environment...

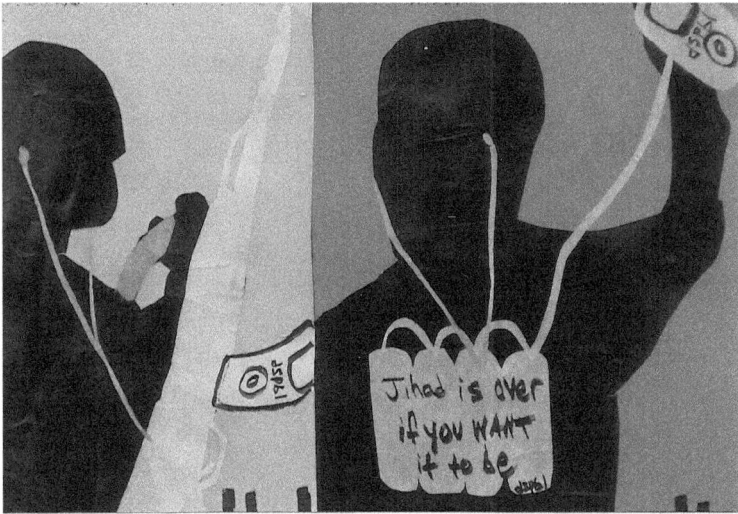

Mandala of Mandela

Imprisoned by the chains of Apartheid,
locked in his cell every endless night,
waited for the dawn of the morning light,
convinced that patience triumphs might,
that a wrong could someday be made right...

This is the Mandala of Nelson Mandela,
father of free South Africa,
brother in blood to America,
"Mandiba" no diva,
his story so real,
no fairy tale
like Cinderella.

He united both black and white,
taught them to love and not to fight,
knew it wouldn't change overnight,
removing a vicious social blight,
now darkest past shines future bright.

This is the Mandala
of Nelson Mandela,
so beat the drum,
sing a capella,
torrential tears fall like summer rain
unprotected by umbrella...

Ubuntu

I am because you are,
You are because I am,
in the intricate design
of a universal plan.
You are there and I am here,
I am here and you are there,
but we are connected
as if we're everywhere.
Whatever I do, I do to you
and whatever you do, you do to me,
we cannot live divided
even if we try to be...

Got to Be Gatsby...

Behind the mask of respectability,
lurks the demon of hostility,
his refined and polished manners
turn into fists like smashing hammers
when provoked by jealousy.
He takes the insult personally,
he can't deflect it graciously,
leaving questions but no answers.
You can't repeat the past, it's said,
and that's a given once you're dead—
Impeccably dressed in the coffin alone,
with all the partygoers gone home,
the mansion's no more glamorous
and the mood anything but amorous,
"Old Sport" Nick's relationship onerous,
his life no longer his own.
He reached for her in his soul at night
across the bay toward the emerald light.
Got to be the Great Jay Gatsby
and his obsessive love for Daisy,
covered for her in the hit-and-run,
took the bullet from the husband's gun,
there's more to life than having fun,
bootlegger's cocktail for making crazy.

Violence of Silence

We searched for the weapons of mass destruction
in Sadaam's Sodom but never found them,
then we sent the Seals to kill Bin Laden,
but somehow, somewhere we've forgotten
the sacrosanct Second Amendment
bears no license for assault weapons armament,
for in the days when it was written,
single-ball muskets were the only guns then.
Now it's Glocks and Uzzis
wielded in the hands of anarchistic crazies—
masked gunmen who invade theatres.

Batman can't save us from camouflaged raiders,
the mentally tortured,
suicidal self haters...
And what about the children of Newtown,
who will help them now that they're gone?
Or the congregation in Charleston
murdered in their church
while praying for their nation?

Who has the courage to end the violence—
the apathy of political silence?

Capital Questions

Do the wrongly convicted
need protection
from the gallows, the gas chamber
and lethal injection?

When the crime is capital
must the punishment be lethal?

Is it justice for the victims
to kill the convicted
or leave them in prison
never evicted?

Shall we heed Deuteronomy
or read Matthew,
believe in the old
or cede to the new—
Is it eye for an eye
and tooth for a tooth
or "Father forgive them,
for they know not what they do?"

Inaugur*ALL*

The landmark 13th Amendment
abolishing slavery
remains, perhaps, Lincoln's enduring legacy,
a monumental act of personal bravery
in the face of hatred, prejudice
and the basest knavery.
It paved the way for the inauguration
of the first black president in a unified nation,
who begins today his second term,
making some cheer and others squirm—
enlightened people wish him no harm,
realizing he's no superman.
Like other presidents, imperfectly human,
charged with the overwhelming responsibility
of the American presidency.

Martin Luther King, Jr. could see the prize;
he climbed the mountain and saw with his eyes,
then he climbed back down and an assassin's bullet
took his life,
just as another one did to Abraham—
Ford's Theater—eighteen hundred and sixty five.
But the dream would not die,
would not be buried in the ground;
more than a century later, the lost would be found,
and not only found, but elevated,
elected, respected—
inaugurated
on the mall for All.

Broadway Run

I am the bullied and nerdy Peter Parker,
bitten by a bioengineered spider,
transformed into a human arachnid,
masking my identity from my loyal girlfriend—
her name is Mary Jane Watson—
the beautiful redhead, the hottest one!
I weave my aerial web, a costumed vigilante
fighting techno villains
in a metropolitan Dante...

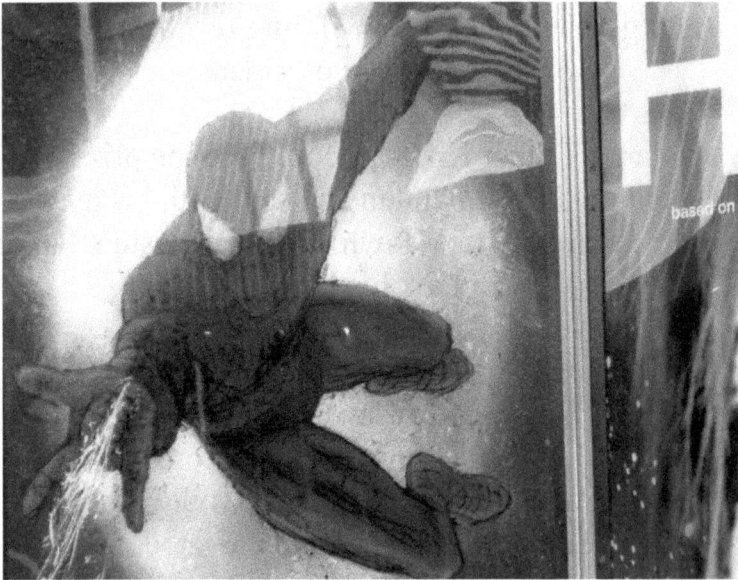

I am the New Amsterdam,
New York's oldest theatre,
restored after decades of neglect
and disrepair,
when the rats scurried through the mezzanine
and the rain soaked the seats,
through a triple-X neon dream
until the 90's when Disney came along,
scored new Tin Pan Alley songs—
from the Lion King and Mary Poppins,
rubbing their magic lamp of Aladdin...

New Amsterdam Theatre in New York City

I am the boisterous Elder Cunningham
a renegade Latter Day Saint
from utopian Salt Lake—
on my mission to the profane Ugandans,
writing my very own version
of the Book of Mormon,
protecting the women from circumcision,
standing up to the war lord's intimidation.

And I am angel boy Moroni Elder Price,
hiding behind a golden smile of nice,
in my starched white shirt
and narrow black tie,
always asking the question of why
I can't live in Disneyland
under the spell of Tinkerbell's wand...

I am the prince searching desperately
for the beautiful owner
of the one and only lost glass slipper,
and I am also Cinderella
riding in a crystal carriage,
looking for a prince's invitation to marriage,
longing for happily ever after
away from servitude
to my wicked stepmother...
but somehow, isn't it always something,
how at the stroke of midnight
the carriage turns back into a pumpkin?
Where in the forest is the fairy godmother
at the darkest hour when you most need her?

I am Guy singin' and strummin'
my song of lost love
on the cobblestone streets
of contemporary Dublin,
meeting the Czech Girl,
feeling the attraction, needing her affection
while oblivious to the reality
of her situation:
separated from her husband, taking care of her
daughter,
providing a home for her friends and her mother;
Still, we make beautiful music together,
but we both know it simply can't last forever;
and when it comes time for me to go,
I surprise her with the piano,
bought with the money me dad gave me,
a bittersweet benediction
to the end of the show...
Once we were one
and now two, twice—
why does fire have to freeze into ice?

You and I are the audience and we are the actors,
we are the producers and the choreographers,
and we're all in this drama workshopping together,
creating live and living theater,
by darkest night and brightest day,
no matter what age,
on our very own Broadway stage.
Some of us are born to be divas and stars
and others understudies,
but we all have our roles to play,

185

none of us are nobodies.
And there's one thing that I've learned
on my lifelong Broadway run:
I can only turn the dark off
if my light is switched on...

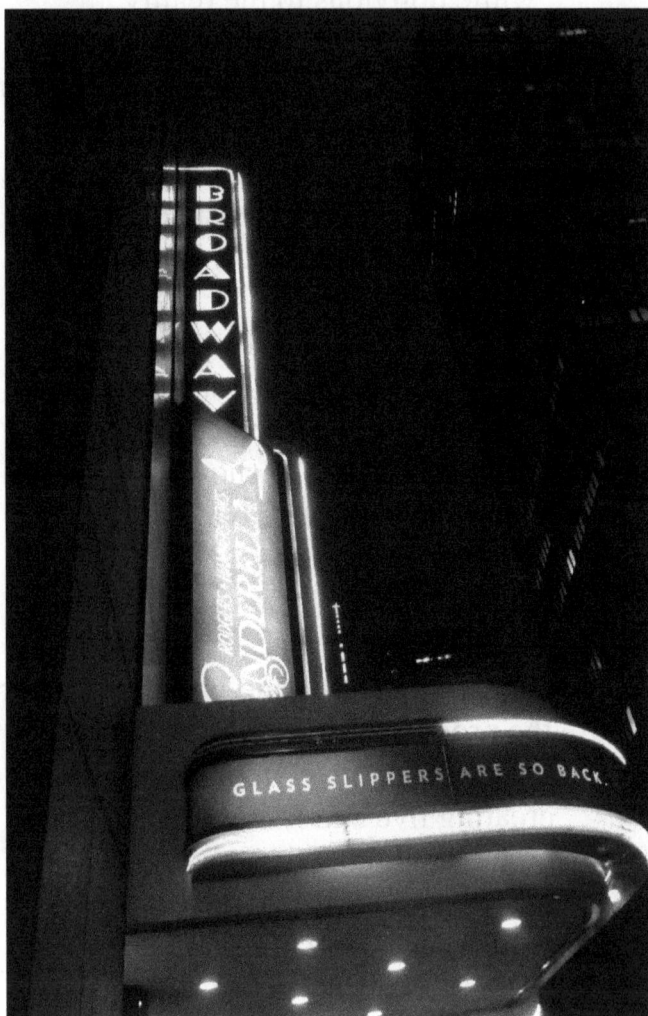

Angelina Epiphany

Angelina Jolie—
a lilting name poetically,
the embodiment of femininity,
but who is this diva,
this Angelina really?

Oscar-nominated actress
Global causes activist,
serpentine seductress,
the ultimate femme fatale,
exotic avatar of normal:

She's more than Billie Bob's tattooed fantasy
or Brad Pitt's red-carpet fiancé.
A daughter whose mother died early of cancer,
Angelina felt the only answer
was to excise her natural appendages of nurture
to ensure her presence in her children's future...

It couldn't have been an easy decision;
nothing is when you're facing oblivion,
your DNA's genetic predisposition.

And all of a sudden Laura Croft tomb raider
became a celebrity pink-ribbon crusader.
It took testosterone's masculine courage
to alter estrogen's feminine image.
Perhaps in Angelina's public surrender,
we're forced to admit and to remember
that only the heart
is the one body part
that determines gender.

Snow Job

Some say Edward Snowden
epitomizes lowdown;
On the run in Hong Kong,
interviewed by the *Guardian,*
was he seeking asylum
or simply a public forum
for causes Libertarian?

No one seemed to want him,
not even Vladimir Putin
until Wikileaks' Julian
in exile Ecuadorean,
arranged his flight to freedom.

House Speaker John Boehner
branded Edward a traitor
but as if risen from the dead,
in effect, Edward said,
"I'm no patriot hater
even though you think I am;
I'm just an ordinary American
whistle-blowing the scoop,
and who's betraying who
when the government's the snoop?"

And what of Private Bradley Manning,
his Army counterpart in disclosure planning,
revealing the secrets of military abuses,
providing his own particular excuses,
sentenced to Leavenworth for 35
while nominated for the Nobel Peace Prize.
Now Bradley's renouncing his masculinity
in favor of perceived femininity;
he wants to be known as Chelsea
and begin hormone replacement therapy.

Should he, like Edward, be considered a traitor
or as an internet information freedom fighter?
The answer depends on our perspective,
whether information's free or selective,
caballed by tightlipped officials elective,
kept from the public to be protective.

It seems like we've been here before
in Orwell's *1984*.
Big Brother was watching,
the clock was ticking,
and now reality supercedes fiction.

190

It may well be impossible
for privacy to exist
in the age of digital;
When we consider the threat of terrorism
we might see things differently
through a different prism,
redefining our concept of freedom.

Maybe all we can do is live transparently,
respecting our innate boundaries, inherently—
the invisible lines we choose not to cross
for the mutual benefit of us...

Now Edward's out of the transit lounge,
the oasis in crisis that he found.
Russia will not extradite him
though Obama would like to find him,
he's free to walk through the Kremlin
imprisoned by asylum...

Frack Out

We continue to rape the land
just because we technologically can,
a phallic fallacy of energy independence
regardless of environmental consequence,
the land at the mercy of corporations and
governments.

Does it make sense
to drill for oil
and leave behind a living hell?

Someday there'll be no well to drill,
an empty tank nothing can fill.

We frack the rocks
extracting petroleum,
leaving behind a seismic mausoleum,
a greenpeace bleeding from the perineum,
filling the rivers with chemical runoff,
killing the fish, unacceptable turnoff.

Somehow we must learn to live sustainably
on Planet Earth where the wind blows free...

F5 Cobra

An F5 Cobra
thrashing through Oklahoma
or turning Missouri into Misery—
when veteran storm chasers
get caught in the crosshairs
and pay the price
with their lives...
retribution of Divinity
or Satan's secret identity?
It's really neither—
It's simply a force of nature,
spiraling in the atmosphere;
all you can do in the future,
if you happen to live there,
is build an adequate shelter
and when the siren sounds
take cover
and if so inclined, say a prayer,
waiting for the all clear,
and when it's over,
survey the aftermath,
see what's left
and always remember,
the same sky that generates destruction
reflects a sunset benediction...

Funny Money

So the government is going bankrupt;
Isn't money funny
when there's no more gold to back it up?
Financial channels just keep it up,
inflationary and corrupt...

It's flexible as plastic,
and elastic and ephemeral,
as instantaneous
transfers digital.

It really has no value than the value we assign it;
it's more psychological and numerological,
logic can't refine it.

Shall we raise the debt ceiling
on a debt-ridden nation
or paralyze society
with political polarization?
And will this partial shutdown
trigger economic meltdown?

The story of money is a funny narrative,
as weirdly complex
as a Wall Street derivative...

Multilevel Devil

Whatever happened to
old-fashioned friendship,
the kind with no strings attached,
with no hidden agenda
under the table
to obligate you back?

Whatever happened to helpful neighbors
who lent a helping hand,
expecting no favors?

Now every meeting,
every greeting
seems at first innocuous
but then turns disingenuous:

"We have a video link we'd like you to see.
It'll make you rich and set you free;
wouldn't you like to come to dinner?
We'll wine you and dine you
and make you a winner,
by becoming our downline
we'll enrich our upline
and we'll be gold
and they'll be diamond,
then you can recruit others to do the same
that's the name
of the multilevel game."

But somehow to me, it's something that seems
a carrot held out to impossible dreams,
a sophisticated product Ponzi scheme,
Bernie Madoff in designer jeans...

The prices have to be hyperinflated
so upline and downline get compensated...

In the labyrinthine details of multi-level,
there just might lurk
the greediest devil.

Bad Seed

Let's reach out our hand
and take back the land,
for we are the heirs
and despite all their airs,
it's ours, not theirs.

We took it for granted
that nature couldn't be patented,
but now that it can by decree of government,
what is the fate
of our vulnerable planet?

GMOS, OMG,
are we slaves or are we free
in this corporation nation's
militancy?

Downtrodden Haiti took the lead
by refusing to plant the altered seeds;
they have learned to live with the weeds,
preferring nature to corporate greed,
burning their plants in effigy.
Are the Haitians indeed,
more enlightened than we?

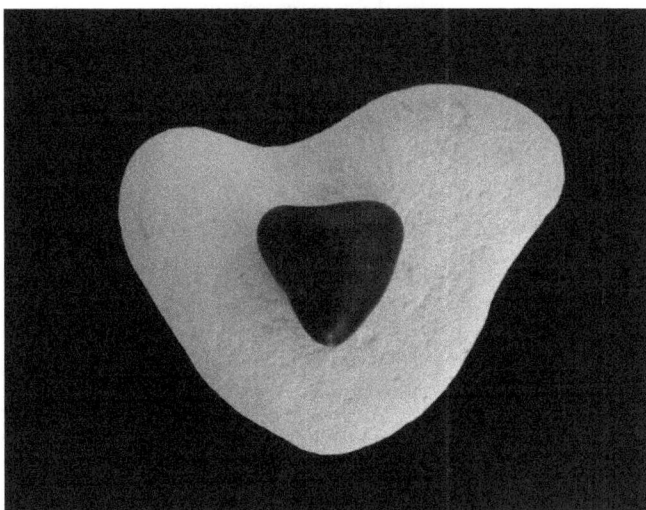

Theatheism

I don't believe in atheism—
it's really a religion
of hypocritical treason.
For whatever you believe in
that's bigger than you,
wherever you go and whatever you do,
that's your god,
isn't it true?

It could be ballet or acting in drama
or paying homage to the Dalai Lama
or unswerving devotion to Osama,
Obama.

It could even be
the bearded brothers of Duck Dynasty,
the right to bear arms and Liberty.

But whatever it is
is another "ism",
a worldview refracted through your personal
prism,
something that opens the gates of prison
and gives you a reason for getting up and living.

So don't tell me there's no god;
just scroll the screen of your IPAD, IPOD
Steve Jobs has gone,
but nothing could be worse
than denying the design of the universe...

Uptown Downton

Uptown Downton
life in the Abbey—
the downstairs staff
serves the upstairs family,
the oh-so-privileged
landed gentry
with their immaculately swept
stable and livery,
their perfectly placed
place settings and cutlery,
respectfully dressed in Edwardian finery.

But all's not well in the well-groomed Abbey
with interpersonal scandal and public
skullduggery.
There's suspicion and fear
under the candlelit light
of the chandelier.
The death of an heir,
his bequest to the heiress,
pretending to protect her,
the lord refuses to accept her—
conflict reigns supreme at the castle.

Bereaved widow is no debutante,
the chief of staff her confidante;
he helps her to assert her rightful position
regardless of perceived social sedition.
It's a complicated inheritance

entailing lineage,
death, love and fortune's
triune marriage...

A maid in mourning for the Earl she dearly loves
tenders her resignation,
grateful for the compensation
he so generously gives.

A dowager's dour adaptability
in the face of change, inevitability.
War and flu exact a deadly toll
but the silver must be polished,
the larder stocked and full.

A footman's letters proving a gay affair
tossed by the Duke into the fire.
A Turkish diplomat seduces the Grantham's eldest
then dies in the middle of their midnight tryst;
the Lady and the maid cover up the evidence...
but Daisy sees their furtive malfeasance.

A daughter who marries an Irish revolutionary,
the Earl never thought
the former chauffeur
was the right one to marry...
and then there's Edith, jilted at the altar
by a man she loved
old enough to be her father...
So many stories and lives intertwined,
class distinction blurred
by crossing the lines...

There's a rescue from the workhouse
and a kind offer of assistance,
and a turning away,
a proud refusal of resistance.
Hiring a valet,
firing a nanny,
the ups and downs of Downton Abbey,
and whatever happens at Downton Abbey,
happens to all—
all in the family.

Haiti is Waiting

Haitian boy with his hand out
already knows what it's all about...

Planeloads of missionaries wearing matching T-
shirts
emblazoned with church logos and do-gooder
words,
but they're not the ones who always have to live
there;
they can leave when they want
with passports to anywhere.

Haiti is waiting for someone to save her
but maybe, just maybe
she's her own savior,
deserving to eat the fruit of her labors
and sharing her bounty with her neighbors
instead of holding her hand out for continual
favors,
because dependency has an unpleasant flavor,
aftertaste on the tongue no Haitian can savor.
She's not forlorn or born as a slave here;
she's an equal child of the Great Creator:
no more black labor
to harvest white sugar!

She doesn't have to be the Caribbean pariah,
worshiping at the feet of the northern messiah...

rEVOLyoution

Revolution: an oxymoron in a word—
have you ever considered
or has it ever occurred
that the first five letters read backwards
leave the question answered,
so you can stop retreating
and finally advance forward?
You must become a lover of you,
that's what true revolutionaries do,
Love yourself first and others will follow,
crossing the rainbow bridge to tomorrow.

The march to the future does not have to be
spattered with the blood of warriors
or stained with the tears of martyrs.
What really matters
is winning the war of the interior
where love and love alone reigns superior.

Life presents a choice between the Beatles
and their message of love
and the Stones and their street-fighting men of
blood.
You say you want a revolution
but you guillotine its execution
by self sabotage and persecution.

Is it more than ironic
the American sniper iconic—
assassin of insurgent Iraquis,
who had a bounty put on his head
because he shot so many dead,
was killed on a Texas gun range
stripped of his G.I. khakis?
Or what about Al Qaeda's Bin Laden
and his zero-dark moment of retribution?

You say you want a revolution,
but to be a revolutionary, we must become
EVOLutionary—
it's the only solution
to revolution!

About the Author

Born in Greeley, Colorado and raised in Denver, James Fly graduated from Denver Lutheran High School and completed a scholarship year in special studies at the University of Denver before enlisting in the U.S. Coast Guard. Completing his service, James earned a B.A. in journalism from Pacific Union College, Angwin, California, then served the Seventh-day Adventist Church with Metropolitan Ministries of New York City, Walla Walla College (now University) in College Place, Washington, the Africa Indian Ocean Division headquartered in Abidjan, Ivory Coast and the Mid-America Union Conference in Lincoln, Nebraska.

Subsequently, he edited two weekly newspapers, the Capitol Times in Lincoln Nebraska and the St. Joseph Telegraph, St. Joseph, Missouri. For two years he was the director of public information for Conception Abbey, a Benedictine Monastery in Northwest Missouri before co-owning and managing A-to-Z's FreshAir Fare, a small natural market and coffee shop in downtown St. Joseph. In 2011 he completed a year-long program in health coaching from the Institute of Integrative Nutrition of New York City. In St. Joseph he served as the president of the Samaritan Counseling Center and the St. Joseph Herb Club and was a member of the St. Joseph Writers Guild, the Midwest Artists Association, the Albrecht-Kemper Museum of Art and the Allied Arts Council, winning a number of awards for his creative photography.

The father of three boys, Eric, Ryan, and Hans and the grandfather of Ethan, Mariah, and Isaac (Eric and Dixie), and Karim and Zayn (Hans and Mona), James resides in Livingston, Montana where he has retired and volunteers for social service agencies and arts organizations.

A Message from the author:

Thank you for taking the time to read my book. I would be honored if you would consider leaving a review for it on *Amazon*.

Check out these titles from
Amazing Things Press

Guardians of Holt by Julie L. Casey

Keeper of the Mountain by Nshan Erganian

Rare Blood Sect by Robert L. Justus

Evoloving by James Fly

Survival In the Kitchen by Sharon Boyle

Stop Beating the Dead Horse by Julie L. Casey

In Daddy's Hands by Julie L. Casey

Time Lost: Teenage Survivalist II by Julie L. Casey

Amazing Things Press

www.amazingthingspress.com

www.ingramcontent.com/pod-product-compliance
Lightning Source LLC
Chambersburg PA
CBHW060920040426

42445CB00011B/719